Stoplights Are For Kissing

Easy Ways to Keep Love in Your Relationship

BONNIE B. DANEKER

Illustrated by Eevie Lanier

Stoplights Are For Kissing: Easy Ways to Keep Love in Your Relationship

Second Edition

ISBN: 978-0-9910032-6-6 (Paperback)

ISBN: 978-0-9910032-4-2 (eBook)

Illustrations by Eevie Lanier

Printed in U.S.A

To George,

My Precious Treasure who makes

full use of the time at stoplights

How This Book Began

Call me a hopeless romantic, but I love to see people in love. Isn't it heart-warming to see them being good to each other instead of screaming, criticizing, or playing the "Blame Game"? You're right, I know. Nobody is perfect. Relationships deteriorate; people outgrow each other; circumstances change. I get it.

I've put in a lot of time to research and analyze the topic of sustaining our loving partnership. And, I've discussed this with my Precious Treasure (my husband of two decades)—and other seemingly happily-connected couples—to compare notes.

The conclusion: If you choose to stay in the relationship, make it worthwhile! The time you have together can be enjoyable and loving. It takes a little effort, though. People ask us how we do it. All the time! They can't believe we're not newlyweds. We work on our relationship to be thoughtful, considerate, and loving, regardless of the circumstance.

Today's busy world has a lot of demands, with work, kids, other family, community, and hobbies. Don't let the externalities into that inner space connecting the two of you.

If you REALLY want to continue the magic and love you had when you first met, I can show you how with simple, shareable ideas to keep you connected. Most don't take a lot of time or money (maybe none) but they require attention and love—and they pay back in multiples over time, as you enjoy a fulfilling, sustainable marriage or relationship.

So, when you have the chance to stop on the road of life with your partner, remember that "Stoplights are for Kissing."

With Love, Bonnie B. Daneker

P.S. By all means, make these ideas your own!

Stoplights
Are For Kissing

1
Kiss at the stoplight

This collection of loving acts is named for a very simple one:

Kissing in the car at stop signs or stoplights when they are red.

When you're driving side-by-side and the law says "STOP", use the delay to lean over for the smoocharooni. The passenger can make the first move to approach the driver. You may want to alert them first, so they're not surprised! It's a great alternative to yelling at the traffic or fiddling with the music. It complements the quiet, eases the tension of an argument, and often starts something for later...

When it's red, pucker up!

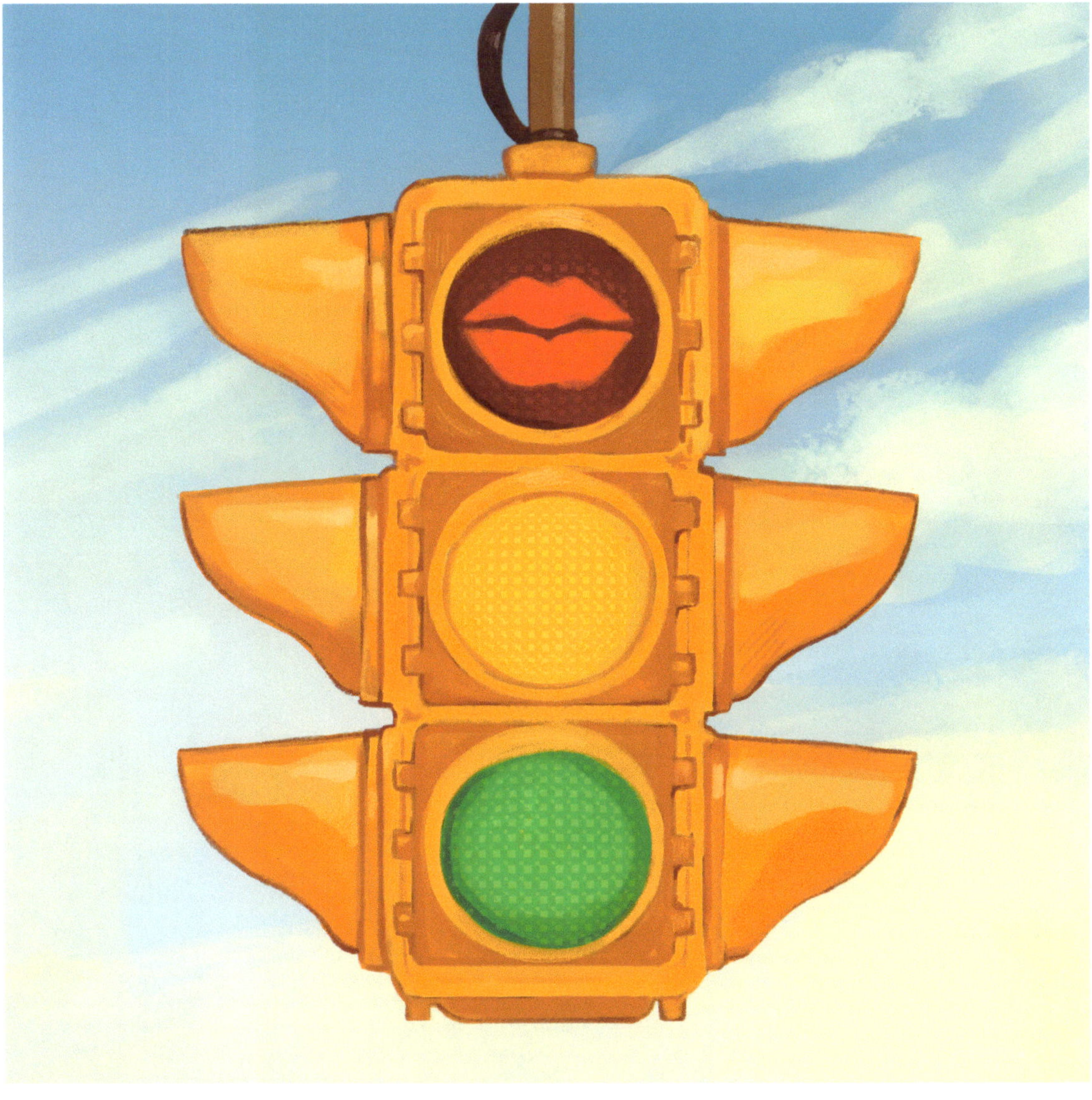

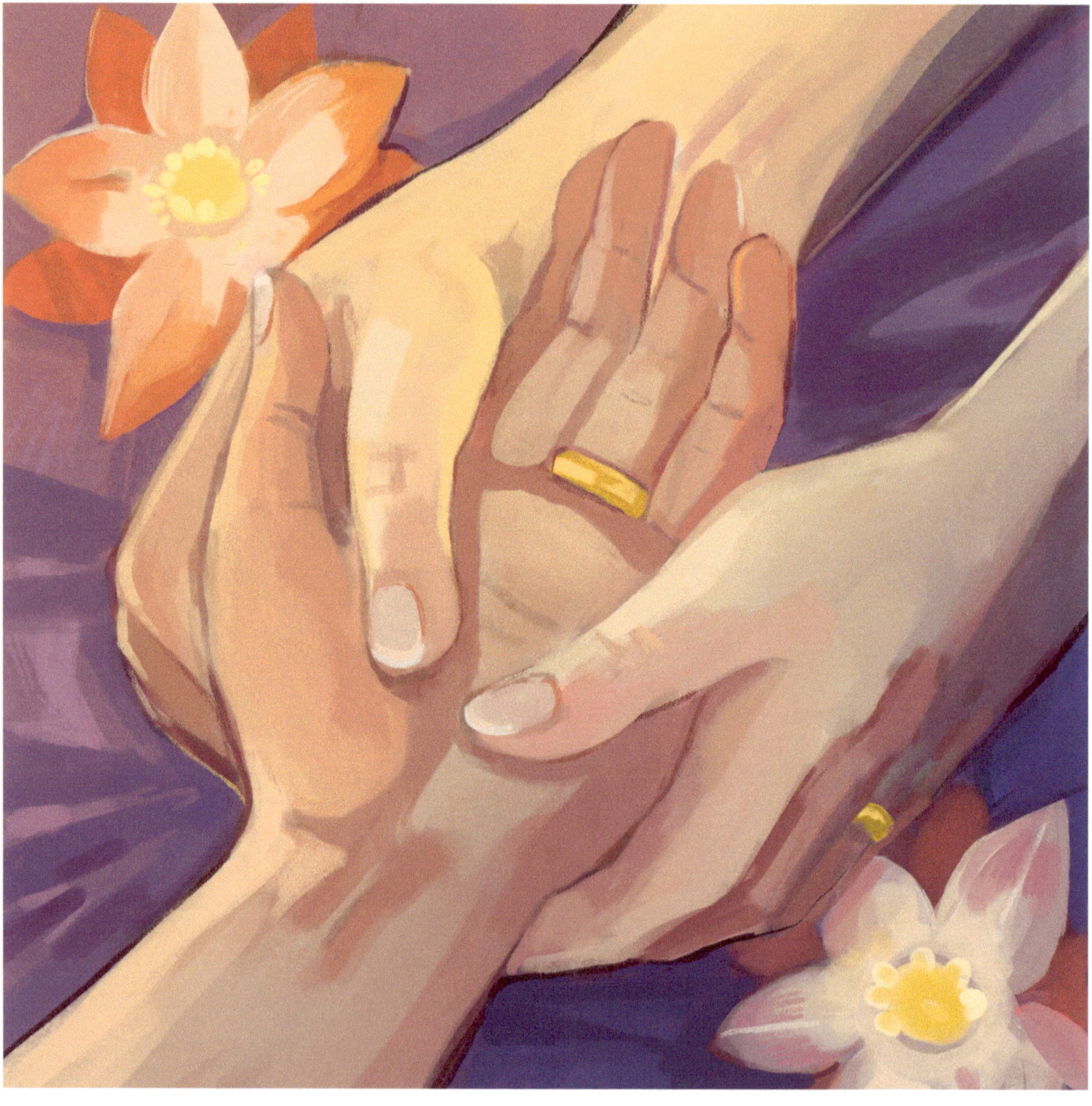

2
Massage their hands

My mother had very arthritic hands, bent claw-like over the years. I would rub them with lotion to give some relief and take away dryness. As my hands age and I feel the aches after long hours at the keyboard, I want my hands rubbed tenderly for a few moments, with a little lotion. Surprisingly, so does my husband! After a long day at his job, his hands hurt, too. We both realize how valuable our hands are, and we need to take care of them. We'll take turns: I'll massage his palms, fingers and thumbs; then he'll massage mine.

3
Start a bath

A relaxing soak can be an ideal stress reliever. It's so great when your partner senses that and gets it started for you. It's easy: Turn on the warm water and put in a little bubbles, Epsom salts or some other good-smelling bath bombs, whatever is on hand. Make it just the right temperature for them. Have some towels and a bathmat close by. Maybe light their favorite candle or play some soft music. All they have to do is step in. Ahhh.

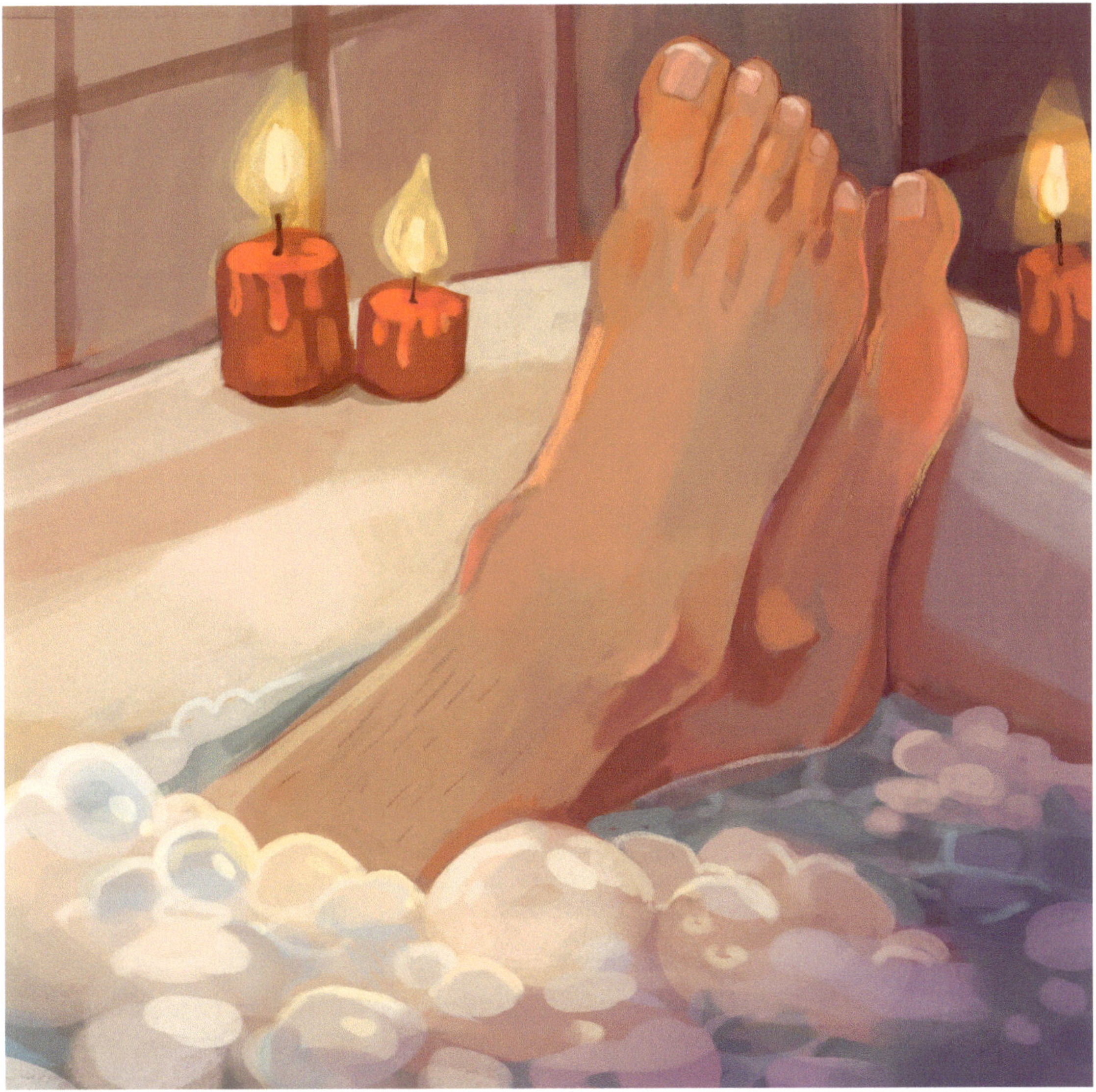

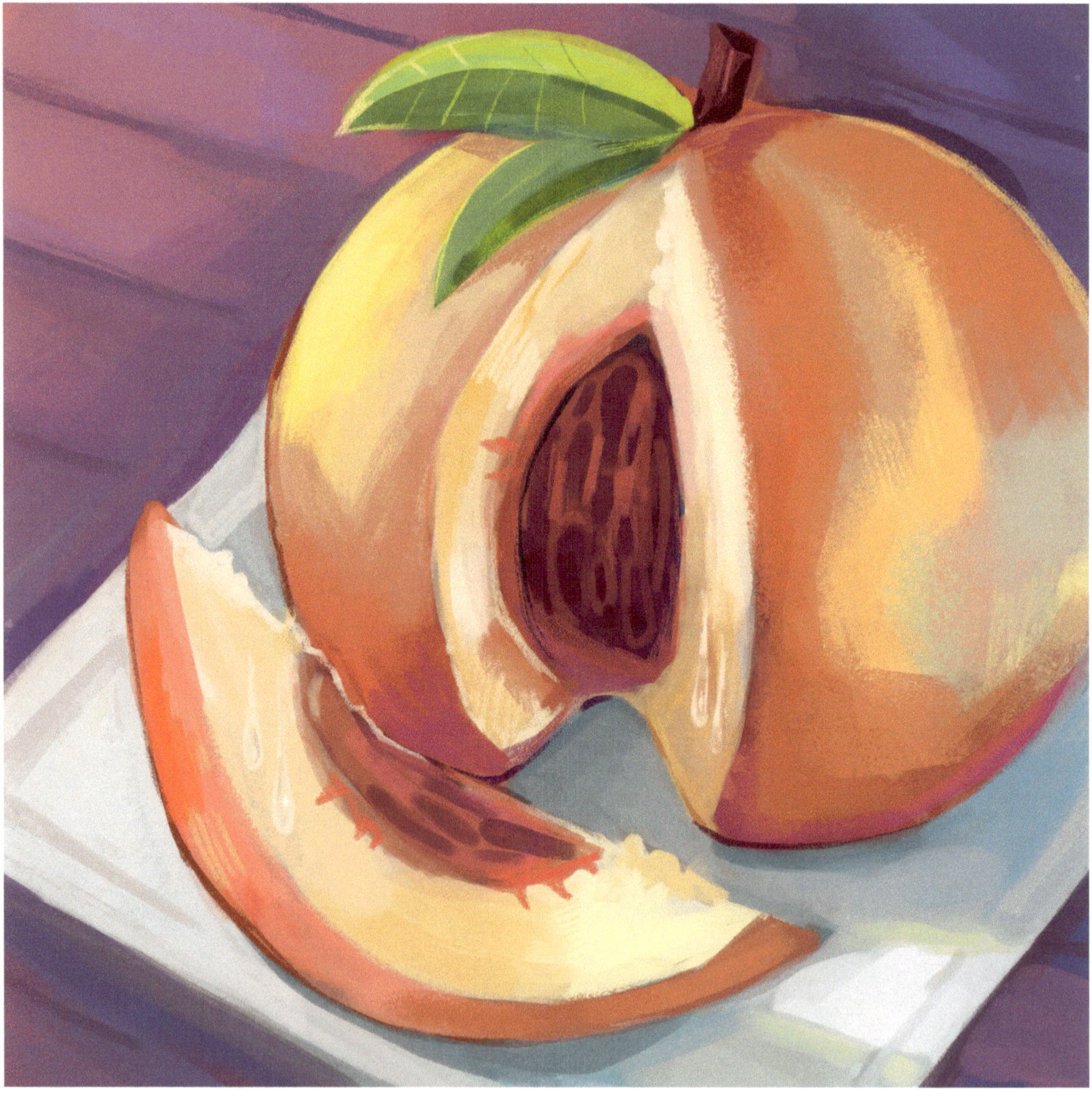

4

Share perfectly ripe fruit

My father worked in a fruit and vegetable market as a teenager. Because part of his compensation was "all he could eat," he learned the perfection points when the produce were their juiciest, flavor-richest. He taught us early that cantaloupes can taste like cardboard or honey based on their readiness when you cut them—and I'm a huge fan of perfect ripeness. I'll put bananas or the pineapple in our fruit bowl for a few days until its peak. I love to share a really runny, syrupy, sweet Georgia peach (and a napkin!) with my hubby.

5

Send nice texts

Who doesn't like those emojis or emoticons? Pictures show 10,000 words they say, and using these take less time. It's really great to look down at your texts see something joyful. Even sending a symbol following your last exchange—a thumbs up, a laughing smiley, clapping hands, a clever .gif or meme—might bring laughter or a smile to brighten their day. Don't discount using the lips, heart, or purple devil, either!

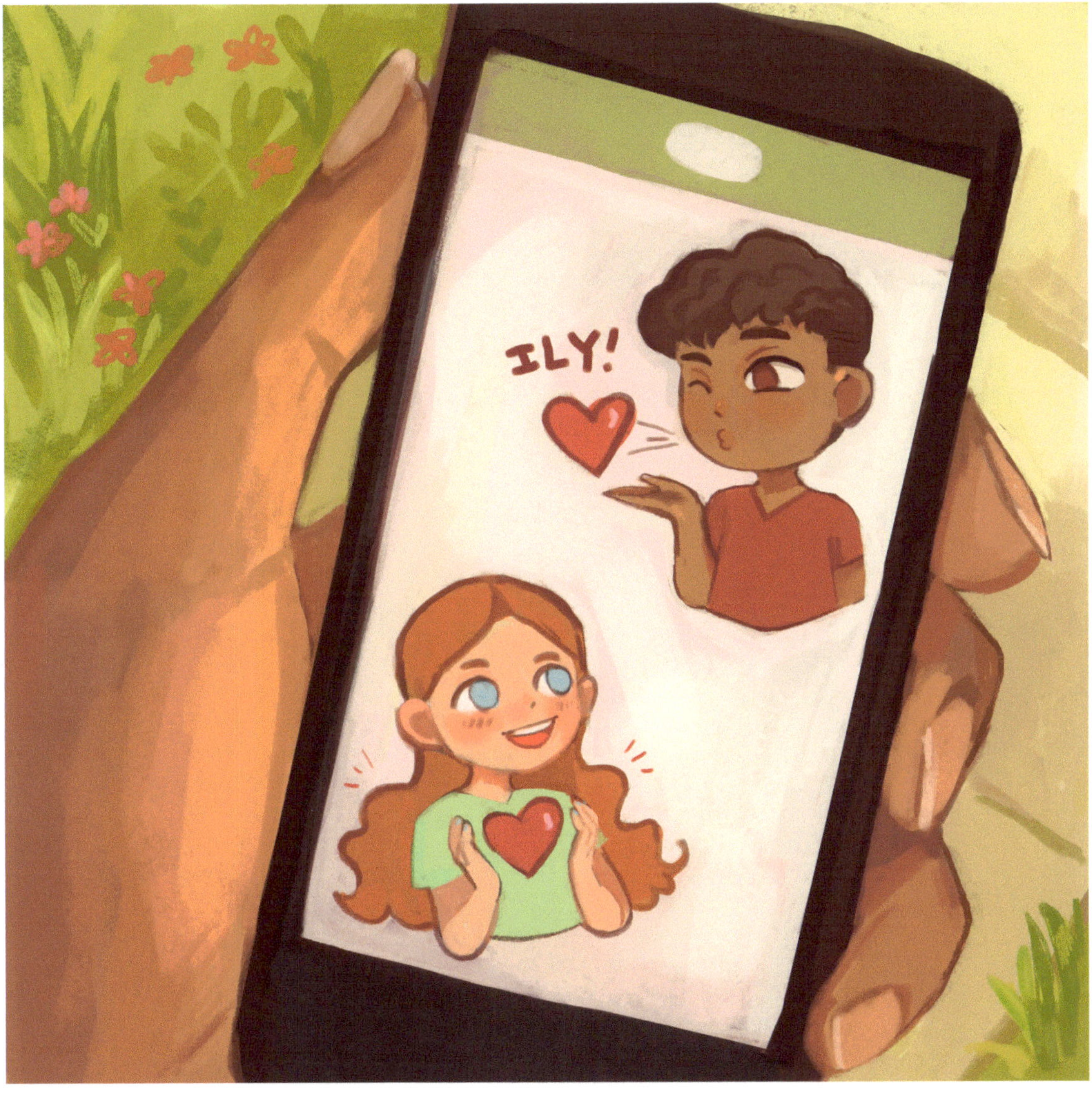
ILY!

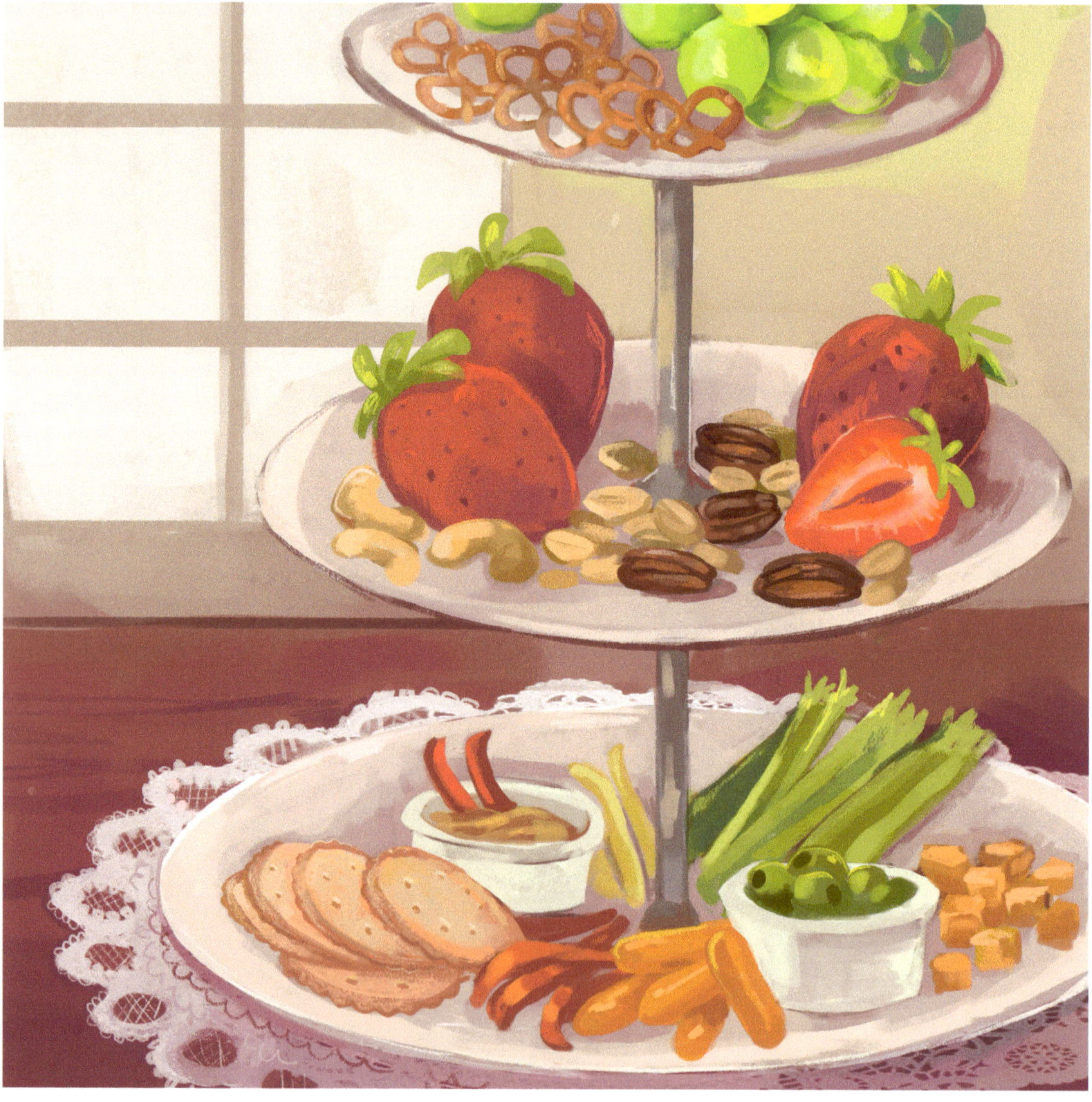

6

Ready snacks

You're ravenous. You'll start to eat your shirtsleeve if you don't get something quick! Isn't it amazing that your partner knows this about you and has your favorite snack ready for you? In grade school, we would sometimes come home to cut veggies or cookies. As an adult, I love dried fruit and nuts. My husband loves cheese and crackers. It's so easy to have the ingredients on hand, and if you can have a small dish of snacks at the ready late afternoon, it just may ward off the "hangries."

7

Hold your partner's coat

Cooler weather brings lots of opportunities to hold your partner's coat while they stuff their arms in the sleeves. This can be especially tricky when wearing bulky sweaters or many layers. When your partner has free hands, they can put thumbs in thumb holes or hold the edges of their sleeves to make sure they don't get caught midway up their arms! You may be rewarded with an extra hug of thanks after the coat is successfully on.

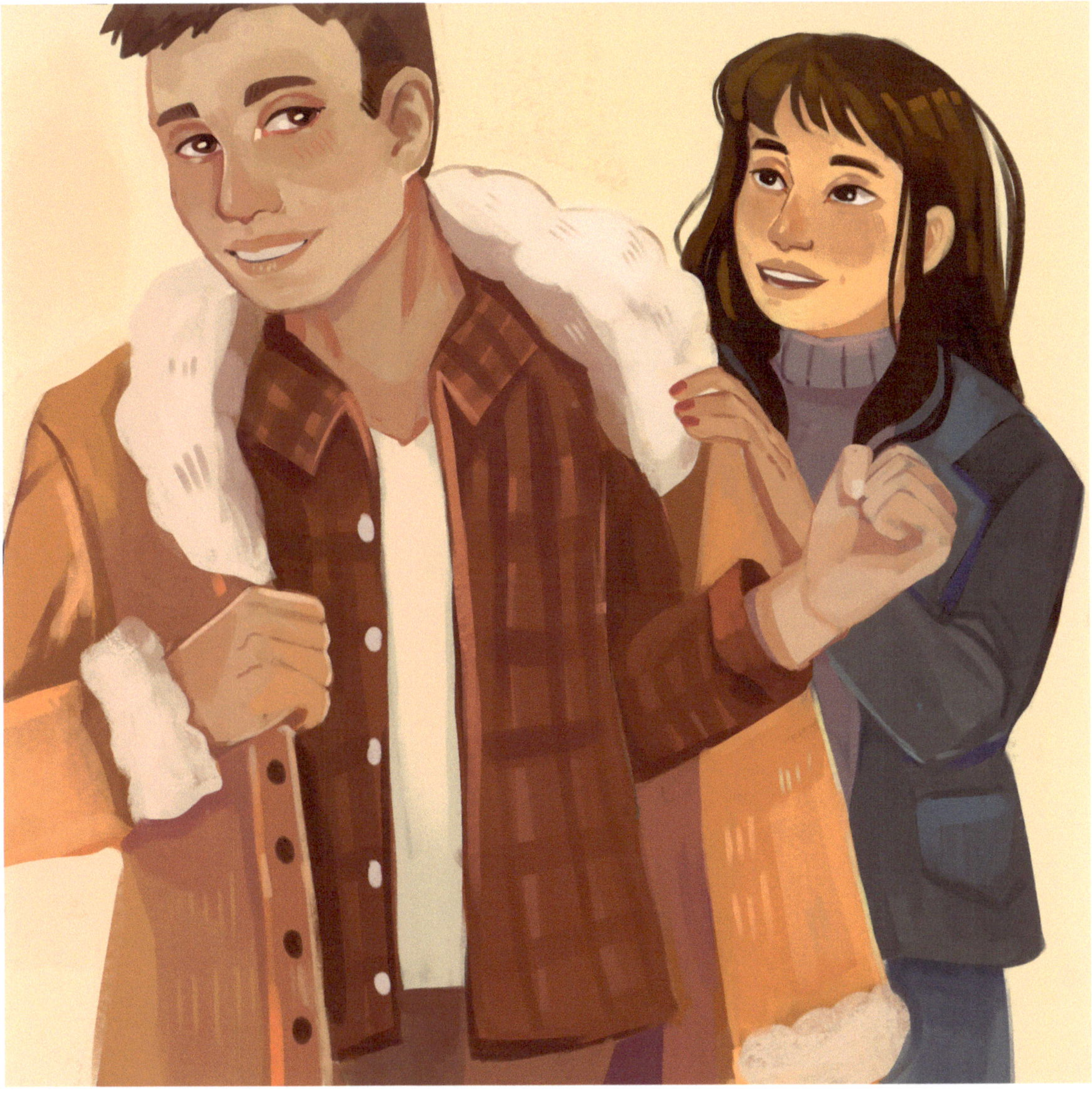

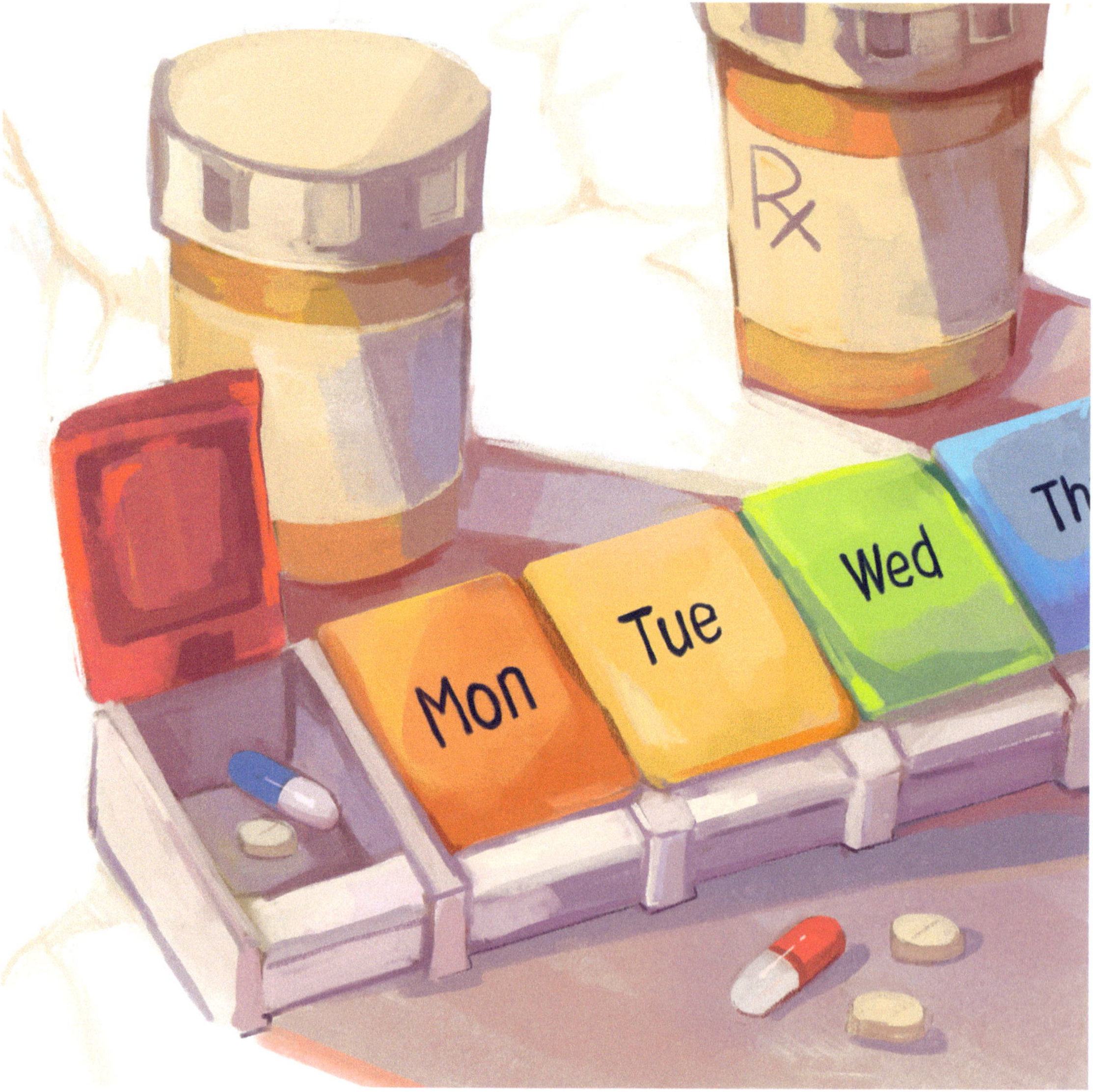
Rx
Mon
Tue
Wed

8

Play pharmacist

Start the morning right! If they take multivitamins and supplements, prepare them for your partner. If you know their prescriptions, set them out on a daily basis, or get a plastic weekly planner at your pharmacy and get them ready for the week. This will help them to remember to take them regularly to add to their healthy routine! Plus, you can keep tabs on what you may need to buy if you're running low.

9

Wait up for them

My parents were married nearly 50 years. For many of those years, my mother would put on lipstick, fluff her hair, and check her clothing before she greeted my father at the door, whenever he arrived home. He loved it. When you haven't seen your partner for a while—days or hours—make a little extra effort to clean yourself up. Then, hug and kiss them when they walk in. It will feel like you just started dating again!

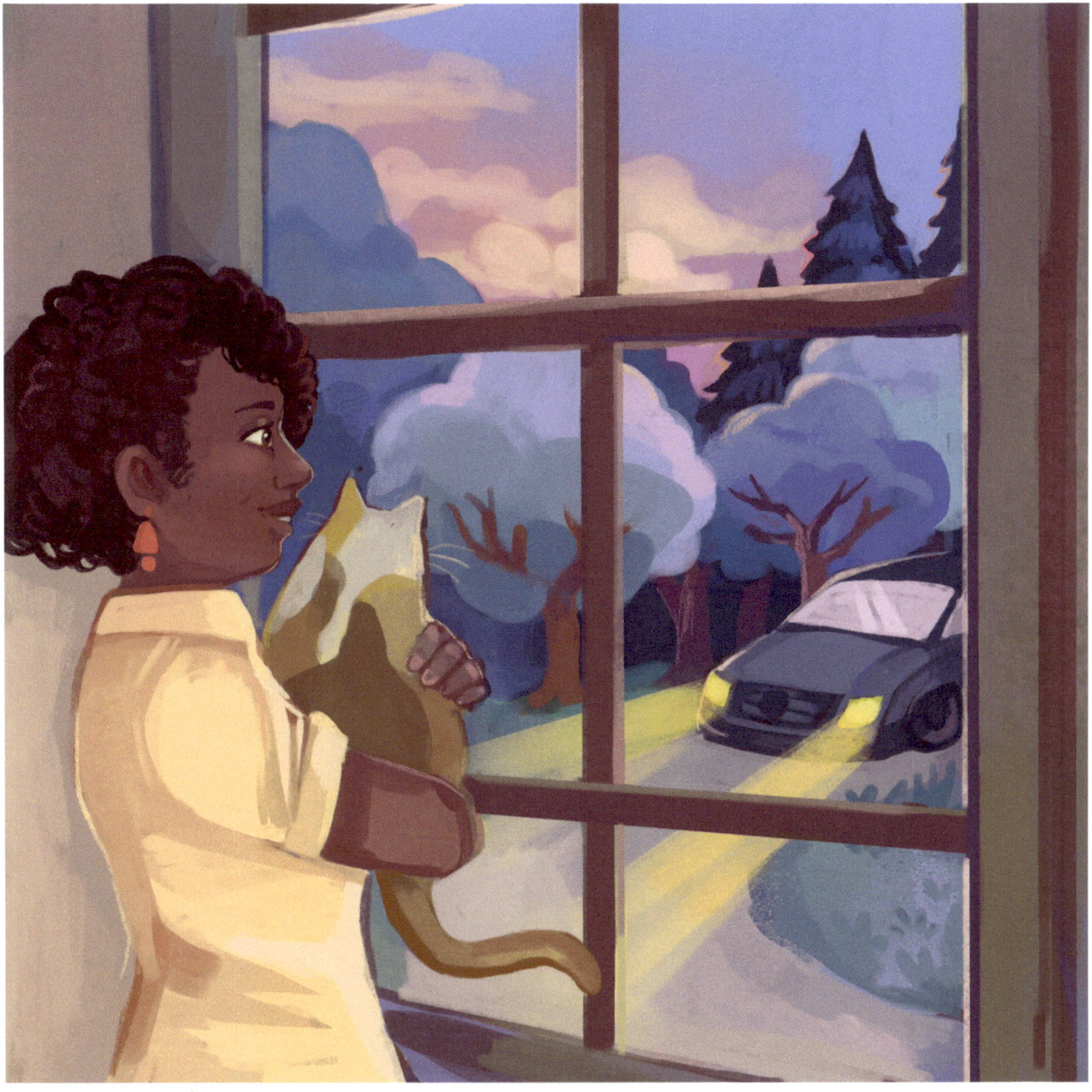

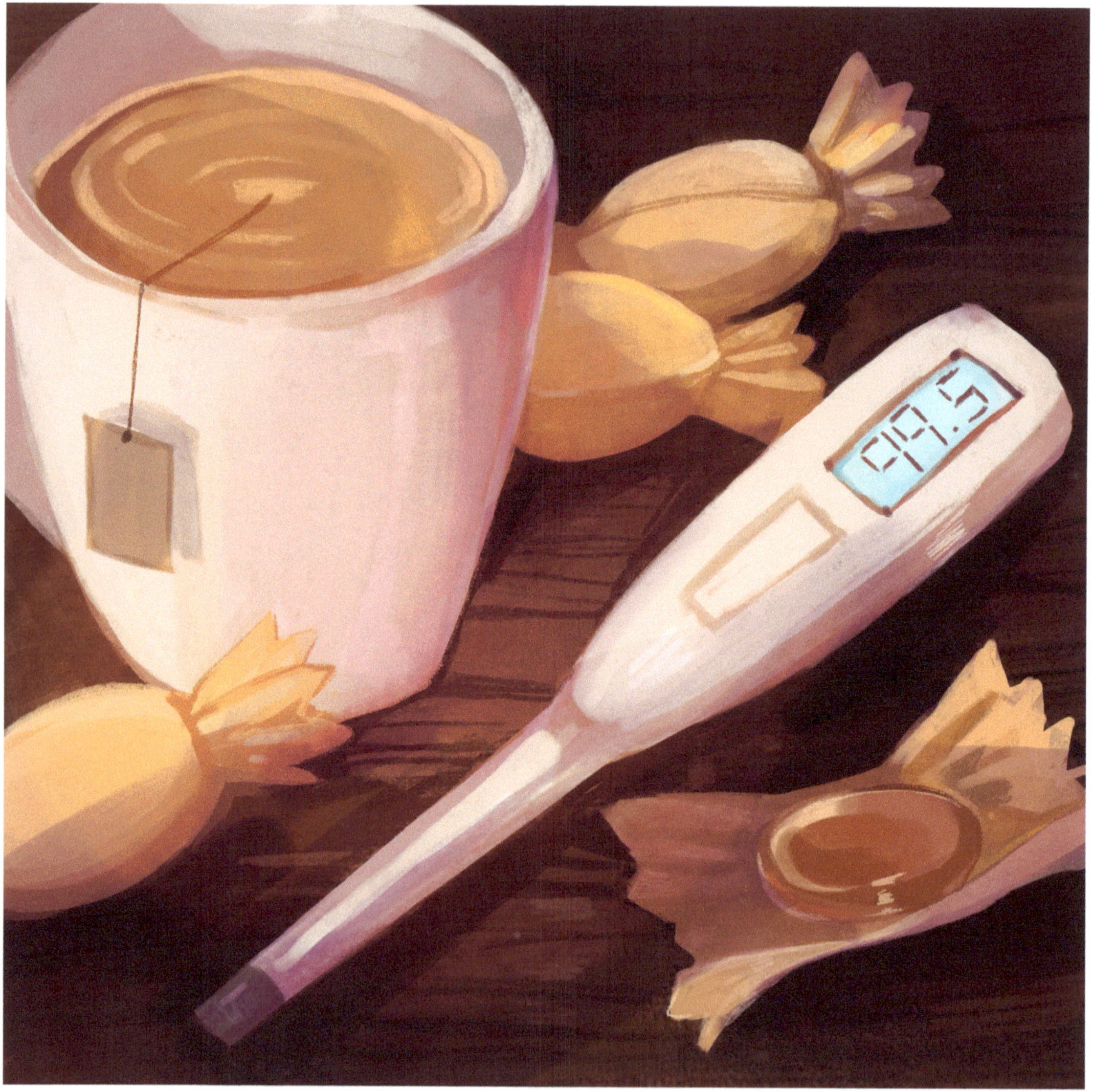
99.5

10

Care for their cold

On a chilly night when you're all snuggled up, it may be hard to think about getting out of bed for medicine. But, if your partner is suffering from a cough or aches and pains, be the loving partner and get up to bring them what they need. They will think you're a lifesaver, and you will sleep better when they are more comfortable. When it comes time that they can reciprocate for you, they will remember with love what you did for them.

11

Clip their toenails

Though it may not be the most glamorous thing to do, nail care is very intimate. Who else touches that part of you but your partner or spouse? Find a sharp, wide clipper for the whole nail width, and catch the cast-offs. To keep them a little "aroma-positive," grab a towel wet with scented soap. This keeps the toes looking good and feeling good, especially in summer months. It can also be in your interest too, so they don't tear holes in your sheets or you don't get scraped in bed.

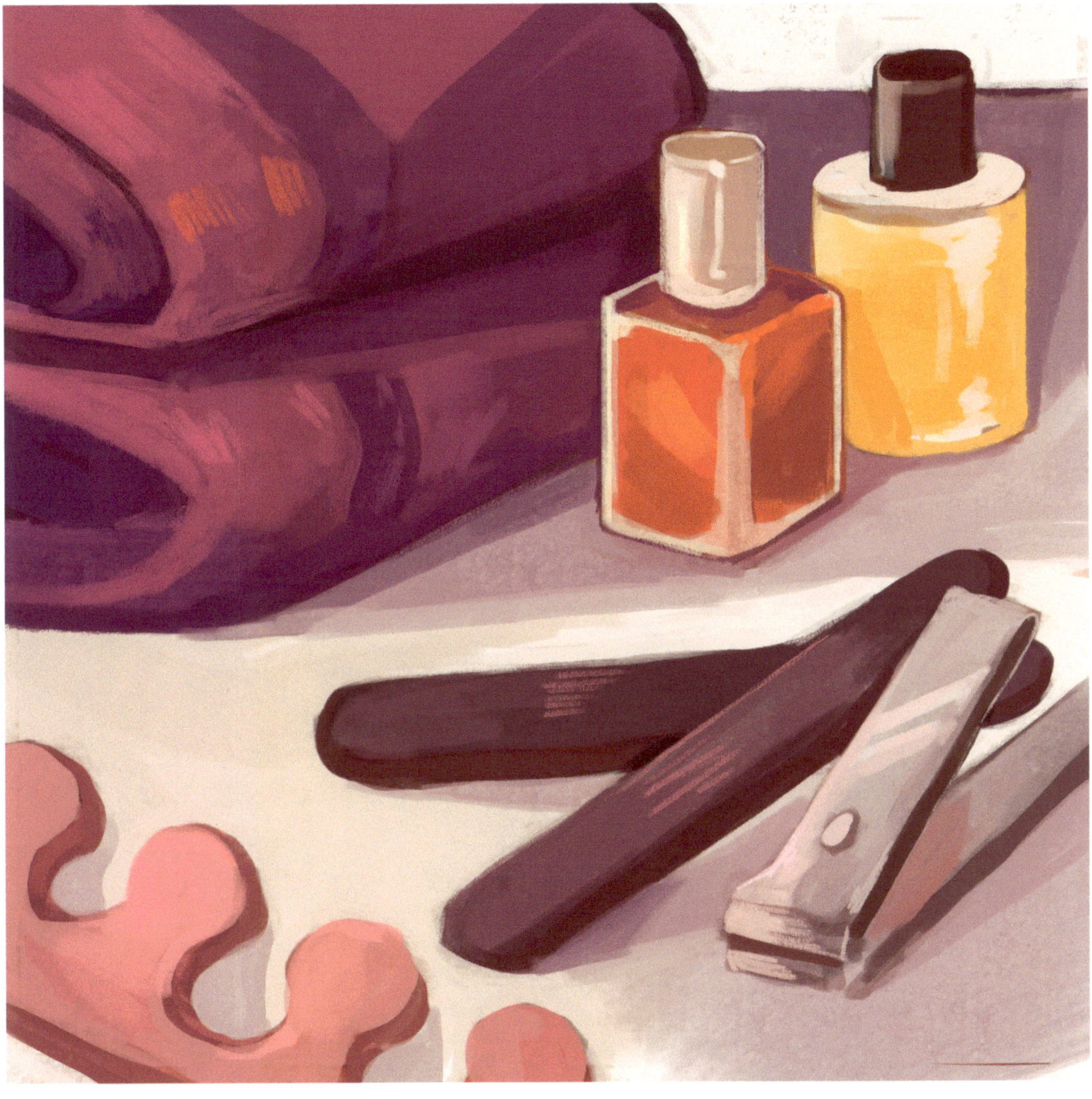

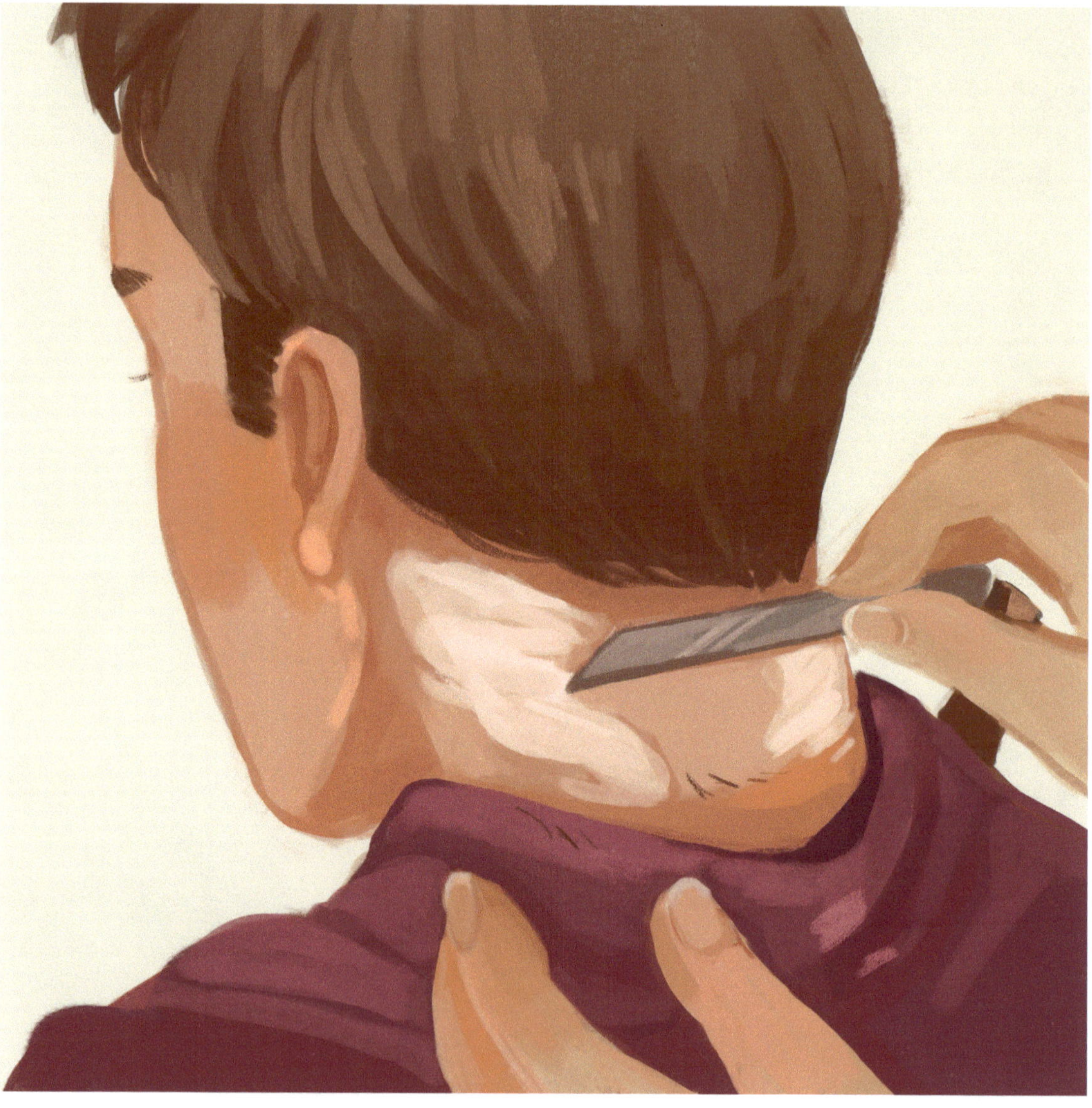

12

Groom unsightly hairs

As we age, we seem to grow mysterious, Malcomb Forbes-like hairs out of our eyebrows, nose, chin, ears, and neck. While evolutionary explainable, they are socially unwanted. What makes it worse is that we can't usually see or reach the offenders! It's a good idea to have your partner trim the "wolf hairs" off him or the "goat hairs" off her. We use blunt scissors, handled grooming blades, razors and tweezers to gently deal with offending follicles.

13

Gamify laundry

I always wondered why, in some households, one person was strapped with laundry duties when everyone contributed to the pile. In our large family, everyone did laundry. When you're living with your partner, it's a good idea to change up whose responsibility it is, or do the laundry together. We play a game of "Fold Five of Yours (clothes first), then Five of Mine." I look forward to seeing my clothes all folded, tucked neatly away as if a genie did them—when it was really my honey!

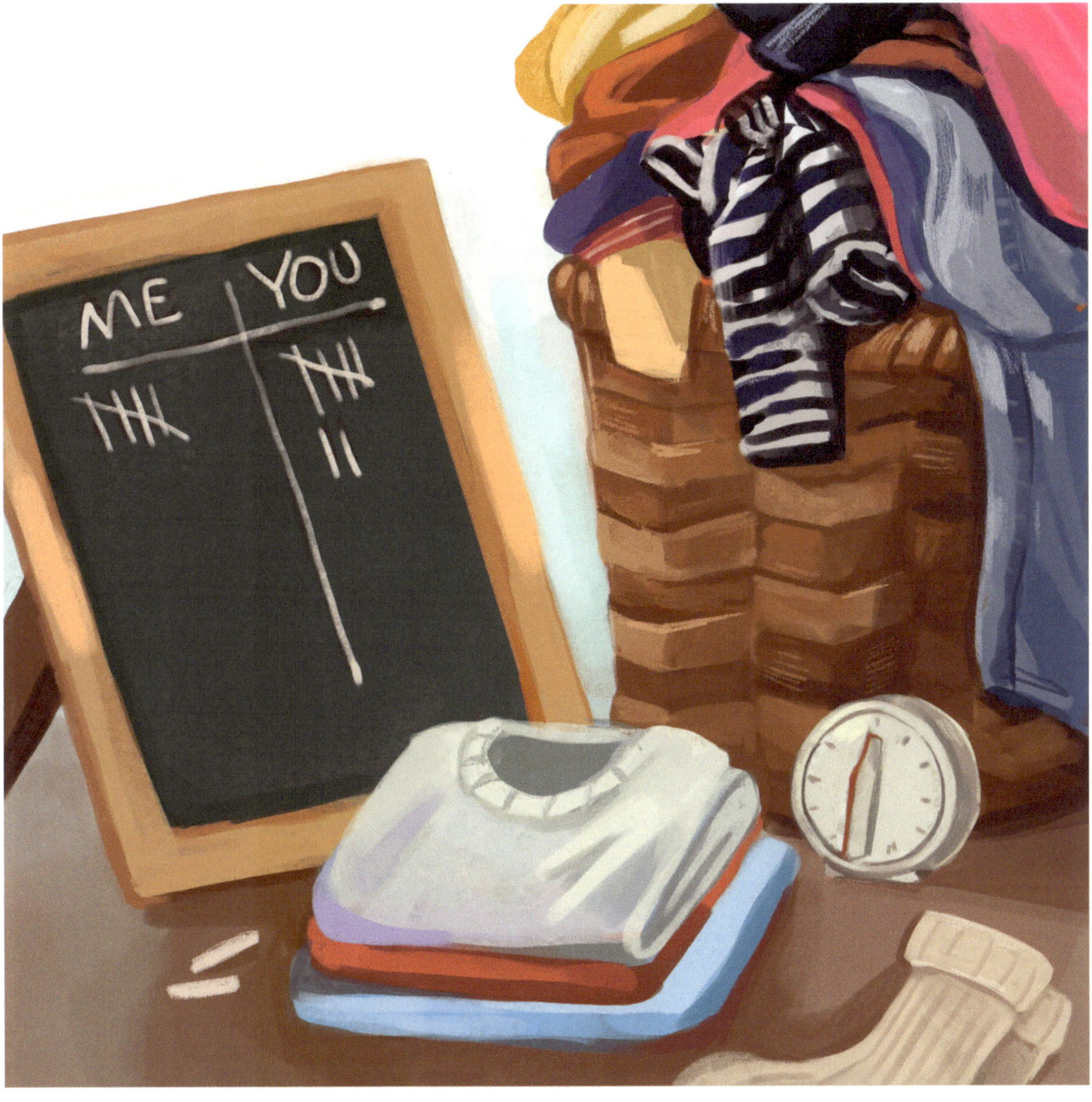
ME
YOU

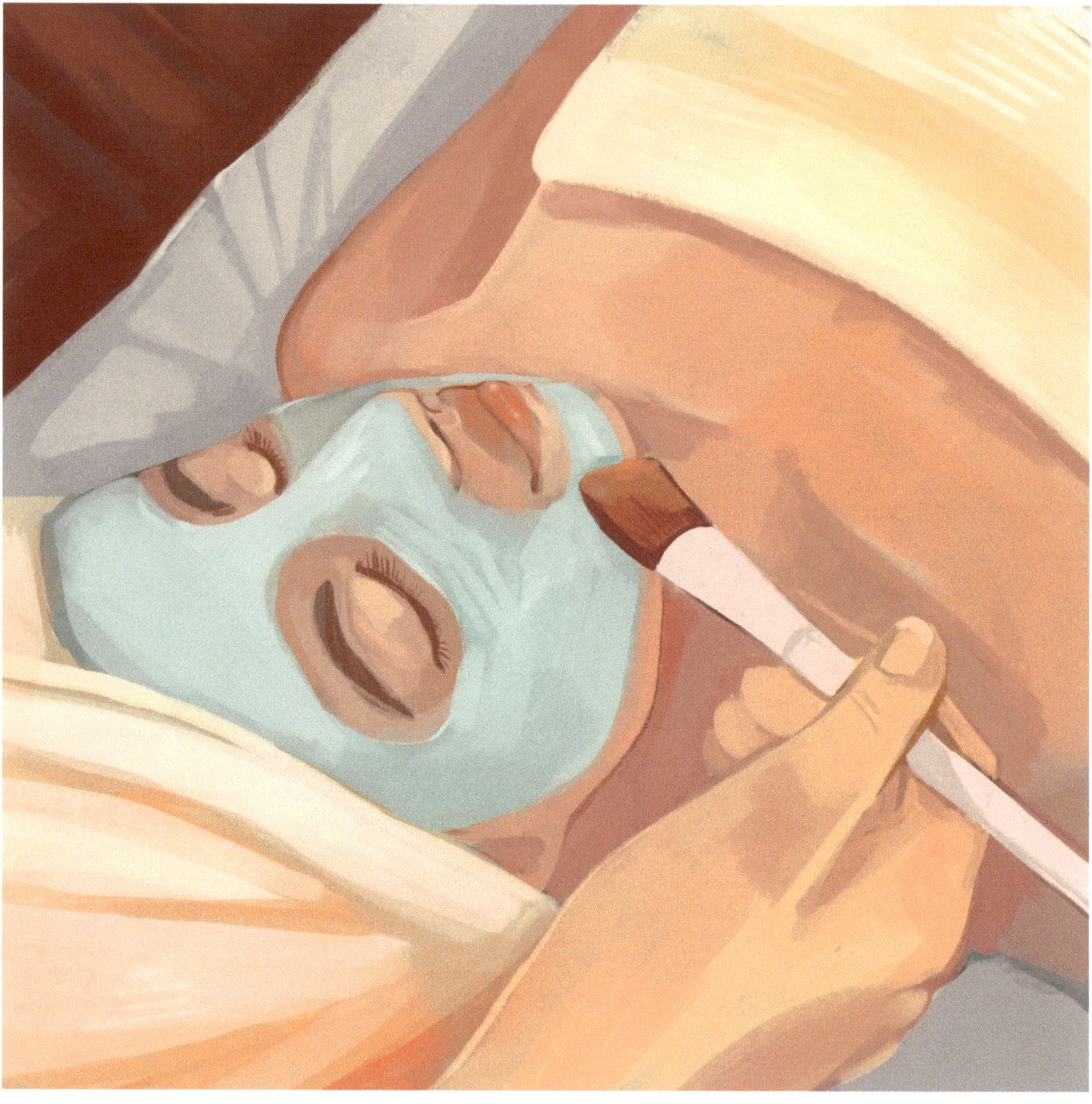

14

Clean their face

If you've been sweating out in the yard, garden, or garage, you can get grimy and in need of a little cleaning up. When you come in, your partner can make you feel a little better with a washcloth sudsy with plain old soap and water, or a wonderful treat of a toner with a cotton ball, or mask to clean your face. It's like having your personal aesthetician!

15

Warm up their PJs

I first encountered this idea from a friend who used to do it for his girlfriend. On extra cold nights, he would put her pajamas in the dryer before she readied for bed, and she would put them on after they were toasty warm. He didn't have to raise the thermostat, and her teeth weren't chattering! Try it on chilly fall nights or brisk winter ones.

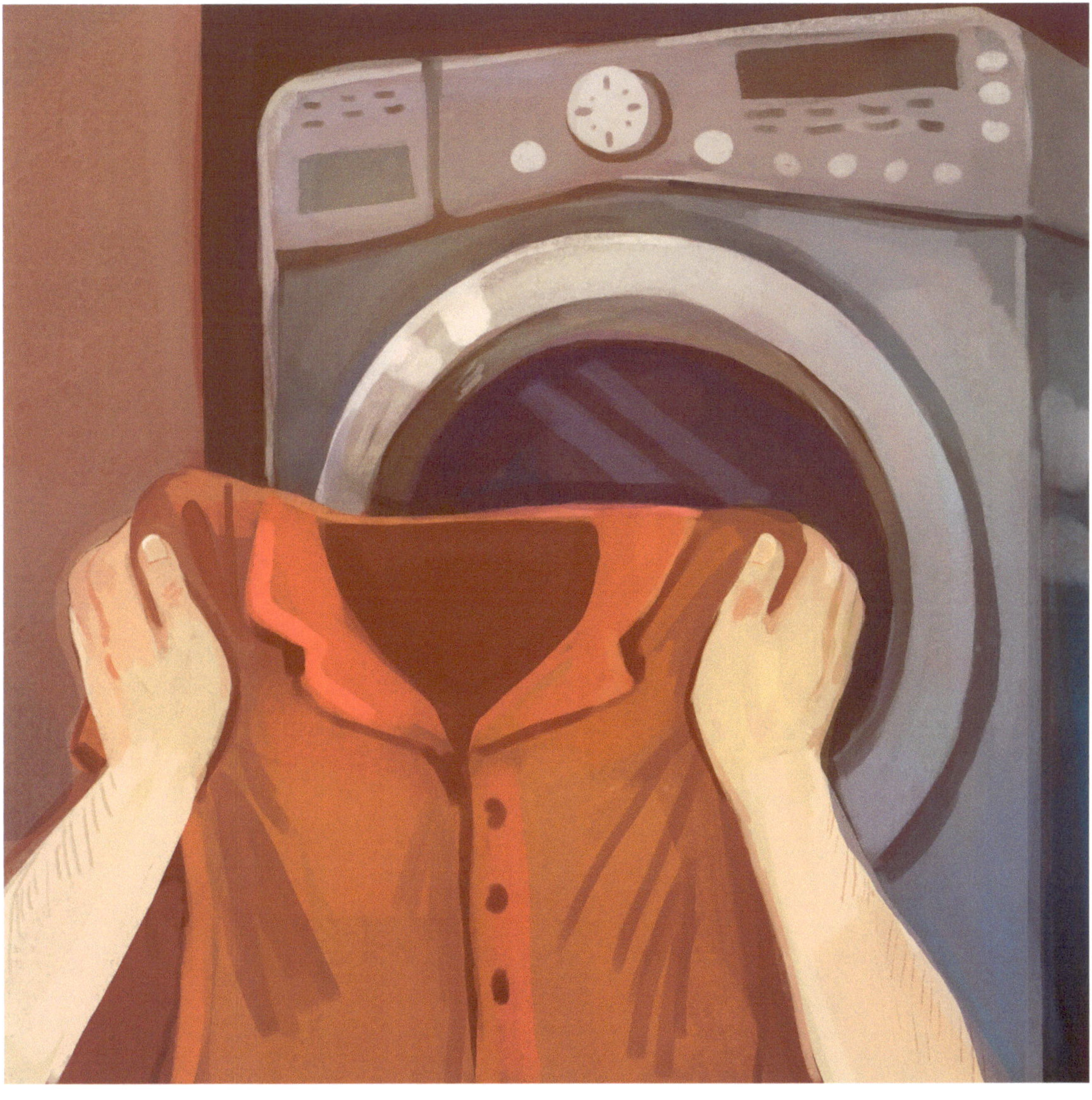

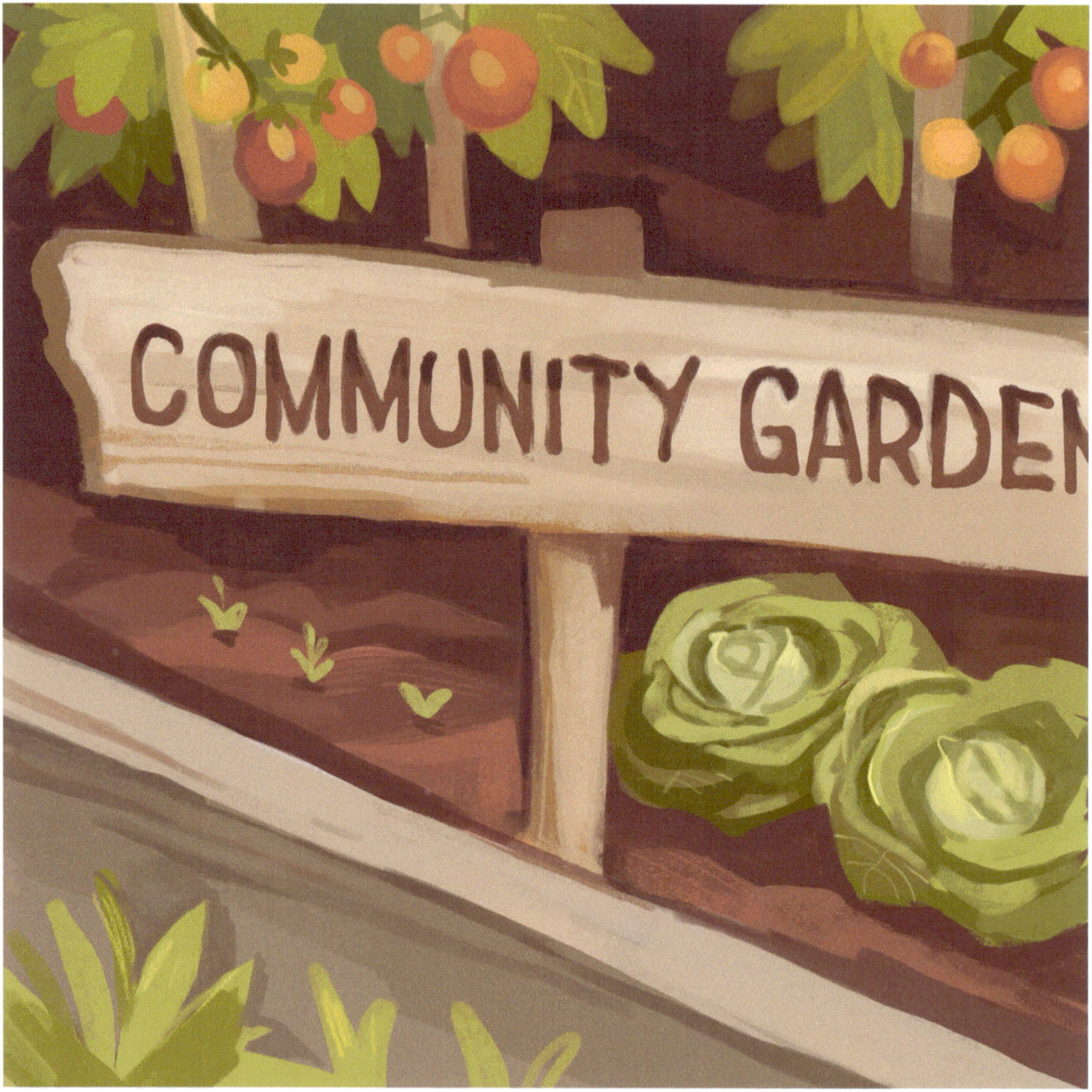
COMMUNITY GARDEN

16

Volunteer together

Your loving, intimate life can extend past the boundaries of your home. A special way to share passions is to volunteer together. Alternate with each other's causes, like pets, the environment, education, children, research or medical opportunities. Most people claim they get much out of volunteering, and this is something you can easily do together to share your love with others.

17

Serve a "beverage du jour"

I'm not sure what starlet was famous for this—maybe
Marilyn Monroe or Mae West—who would greet her
gentleman caller with his drink of choice. In our house, we've
broadened the gesture to both partners. The rule: whoever's
home first gets the choice to make it or not, depending on
schedule demands. Occasionally, we bring the "beverage
du jour" to the airport when we pick each other up. Even
if it's ice water, this is a tradition worth continuing.

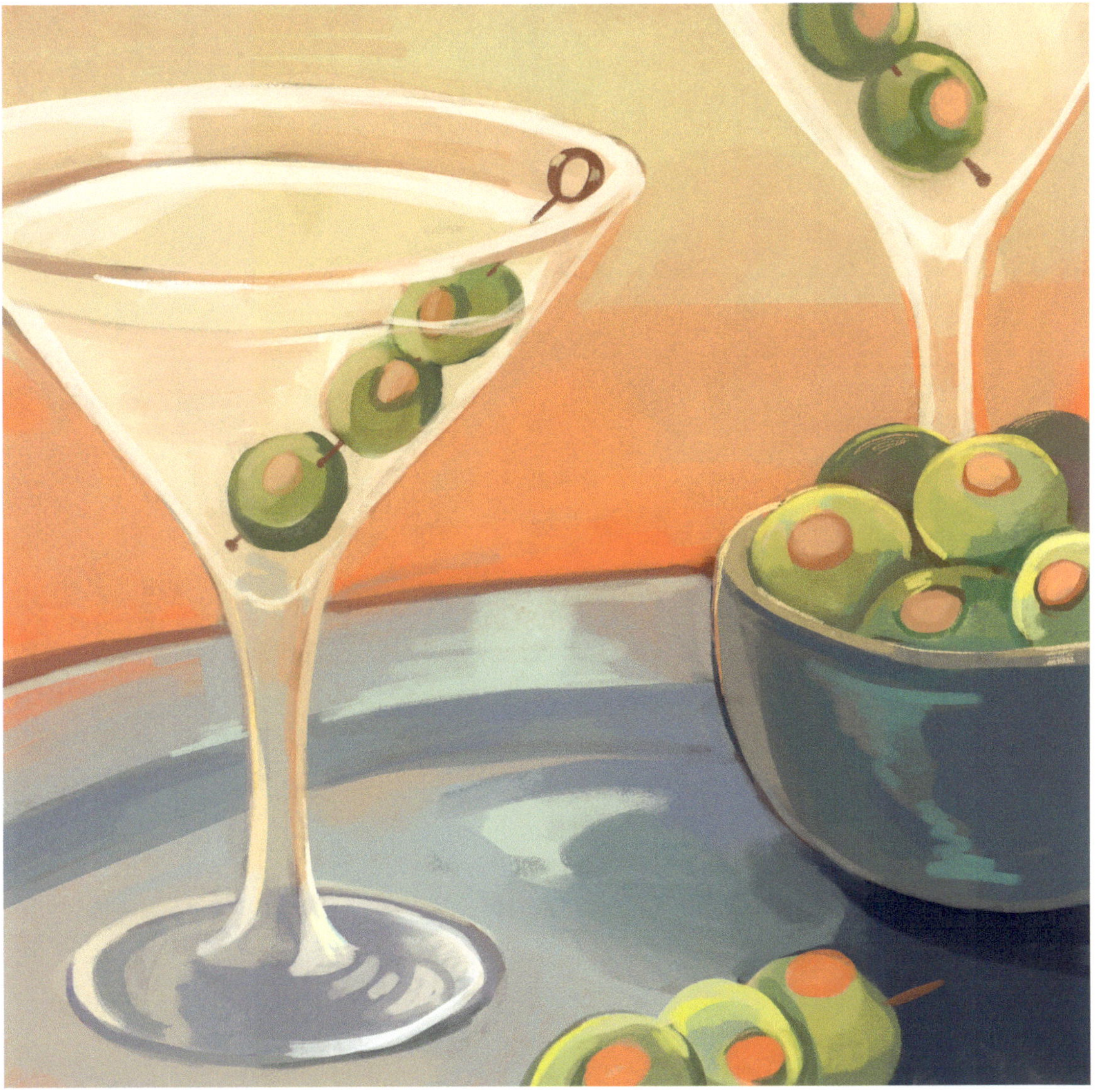

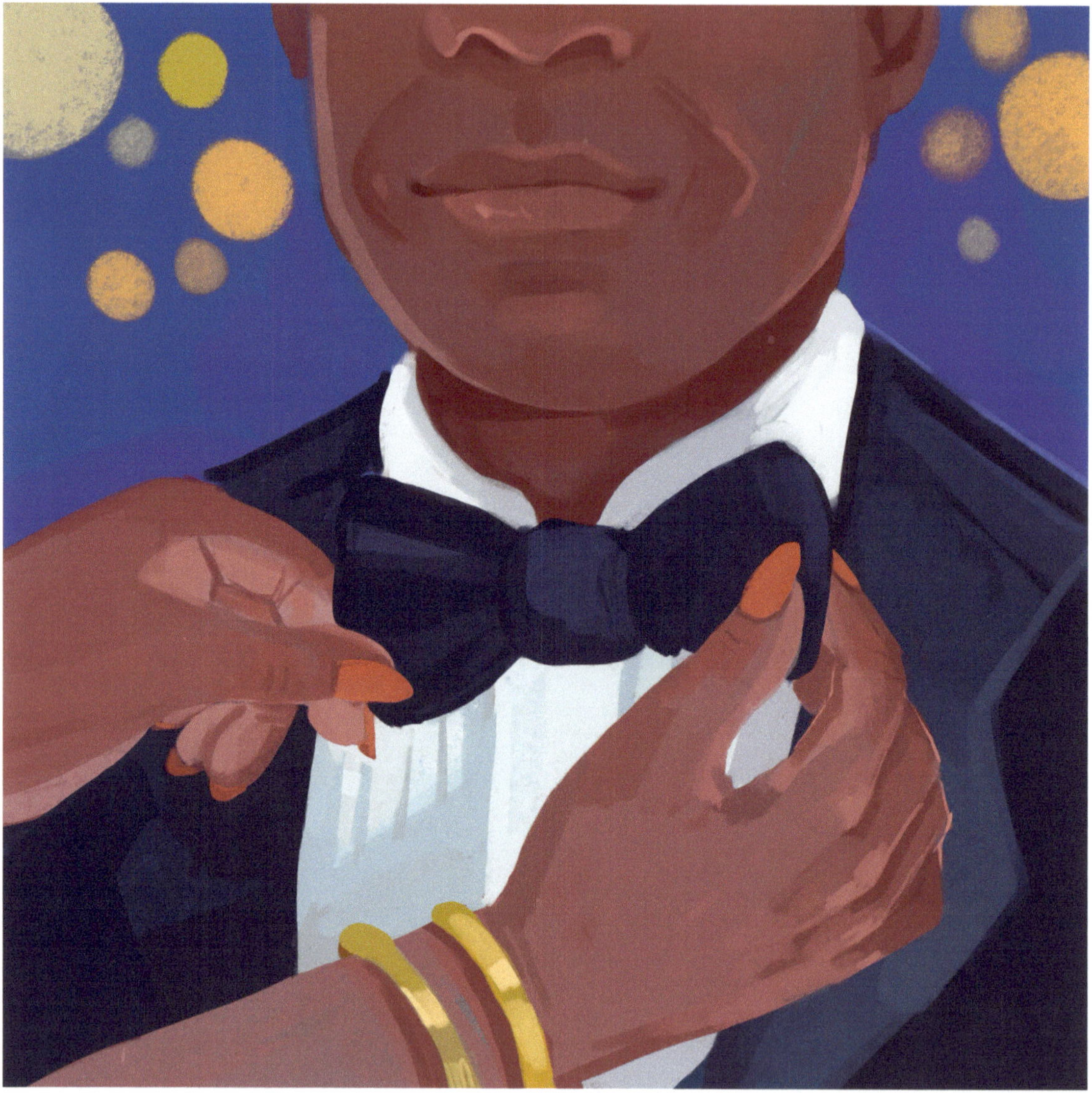

18

Fix important details

Most of us don't wear ball gowns or tuxedos every day. When an important day arrives and it's time to shimmy into that grand apparel, we may be out of practice. Line up his suspenders or cummerbund, perk-up the bow tie, and orient the studs. Tie a sash or ribbons, pull down the dress lining, or pin her throw. You can make each other look like royalty.

19

Create intimate nicknames

You know what I'm talking about: terms of endearment. Some are casual and usual, like "honey" or "sweetheart," but others are very personal—known between just the two of you. No one needs to know them, how they originated, or what they mean. They are special. I won't share ours here; I'll let you wonder instead about what names you can give to your lovey.

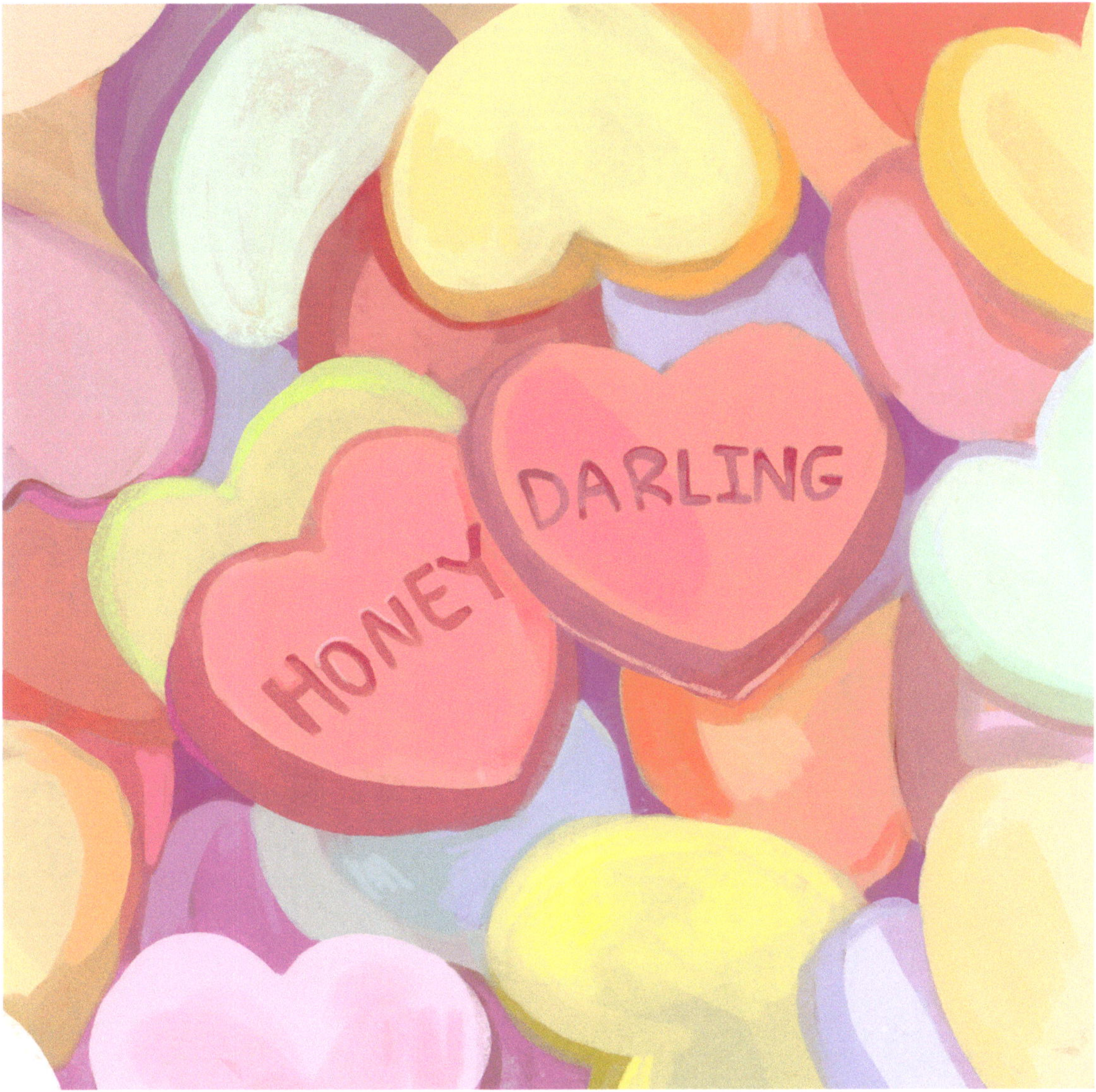
HONEY
DARLING

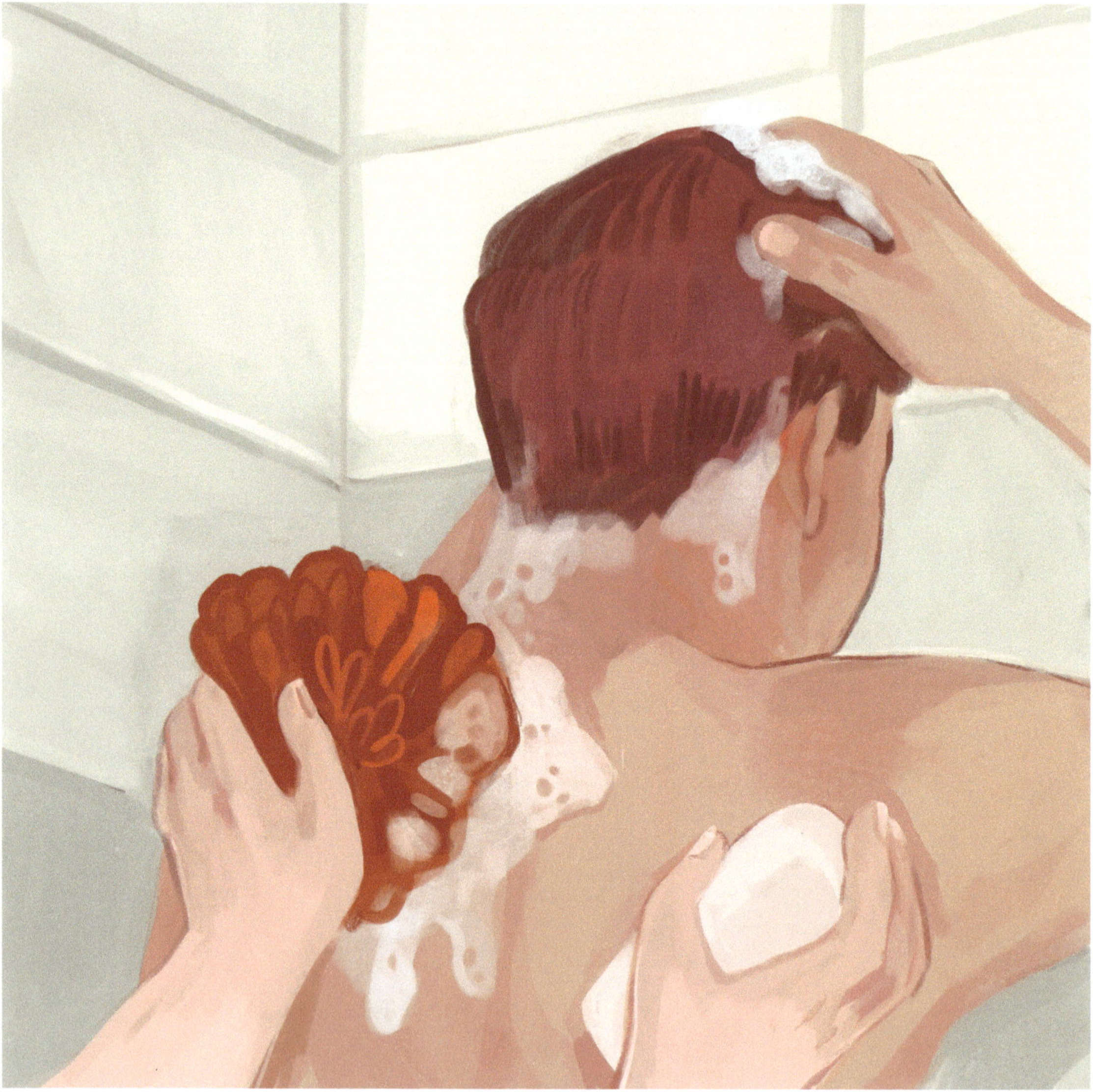

20

Scrub each other's backs

Near the top of the intimacy list is standing together in steam, lovingly touching each other. When showering with your partner, shampoo and condition their hair or scalp, and let the suds run down. Ask your partner to turn their body around to use exfoliation gloves, a scrub, or a loofah to slough off the roughness of their back. Take your time during this great pleasure and have them return the favor.

21

Sing to each other, even off-key

Not all of us are born with voices like a Carolina Wren, but all of us can try to sing cute little rhymes or songs to our partners. It's especially meaningful if you personalize song lyrics. My husband will sing the "I Do!" lyric of a country song: "Every time I try to tell her how I feel, it comes out 'I love you'" (and in the background comes, "I Do!"). It makes me smile every time I hear that song played, whether he is with me or not.

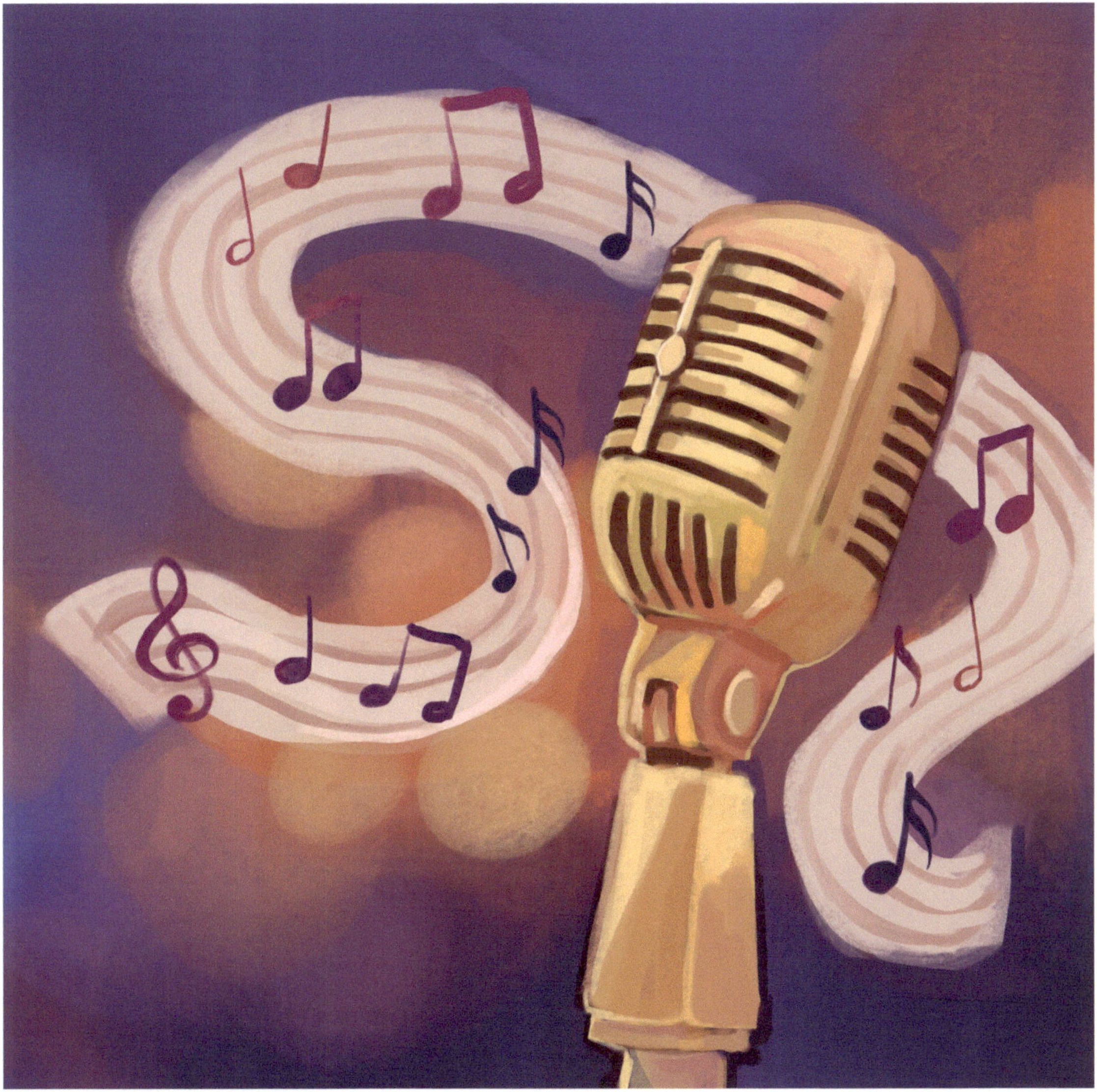

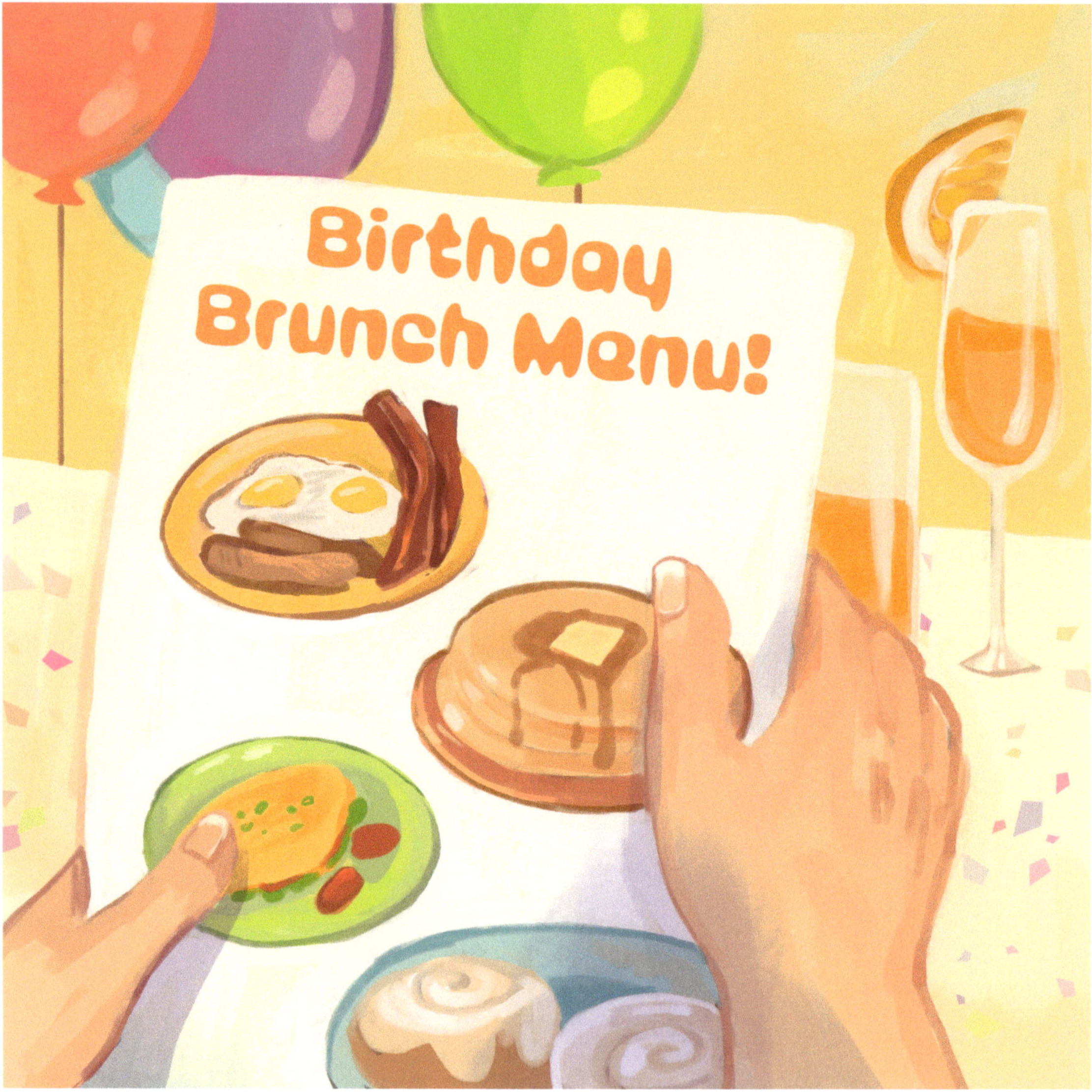
Birthday
Brunch Menu!

22

Plan a special meal

Whether it's a birthday, a promotion, or another accomplishment, preparing a meal that's a feast for the senses is something we can all treasure. When you plan it, think through how it will look and smell, in addition to how it will taste, for extra pleasure. This also works to help your partner feel better after hearing some tough news. Being waited on and served delicious food, no matter how simple, is delightful.

23

Put toothpaste on their toothbrush

My sister would load her toothbrush, then her daughter's, before they brushed together. Even as a small child, she never had to remind her daughter to brush, which led to quality time with her even as a teenager. This works for couples too. We load up the toothbrushes (whoever gets in the bathroom first) as a way of saying "I'm thinking about you!" If you share this night-time routine, you can also have a lively discussion on which kind to buy beforehand—paste or gel!

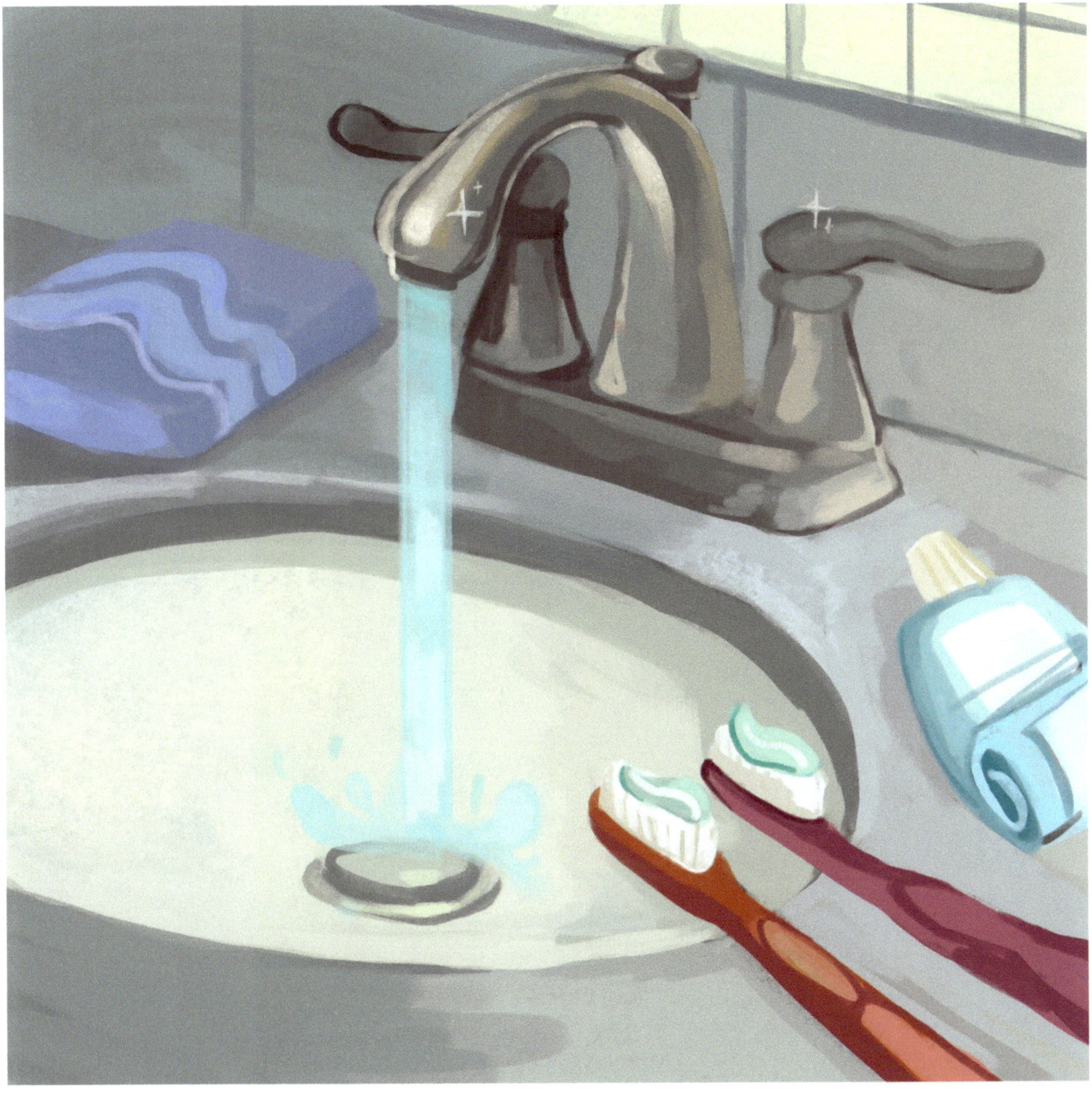

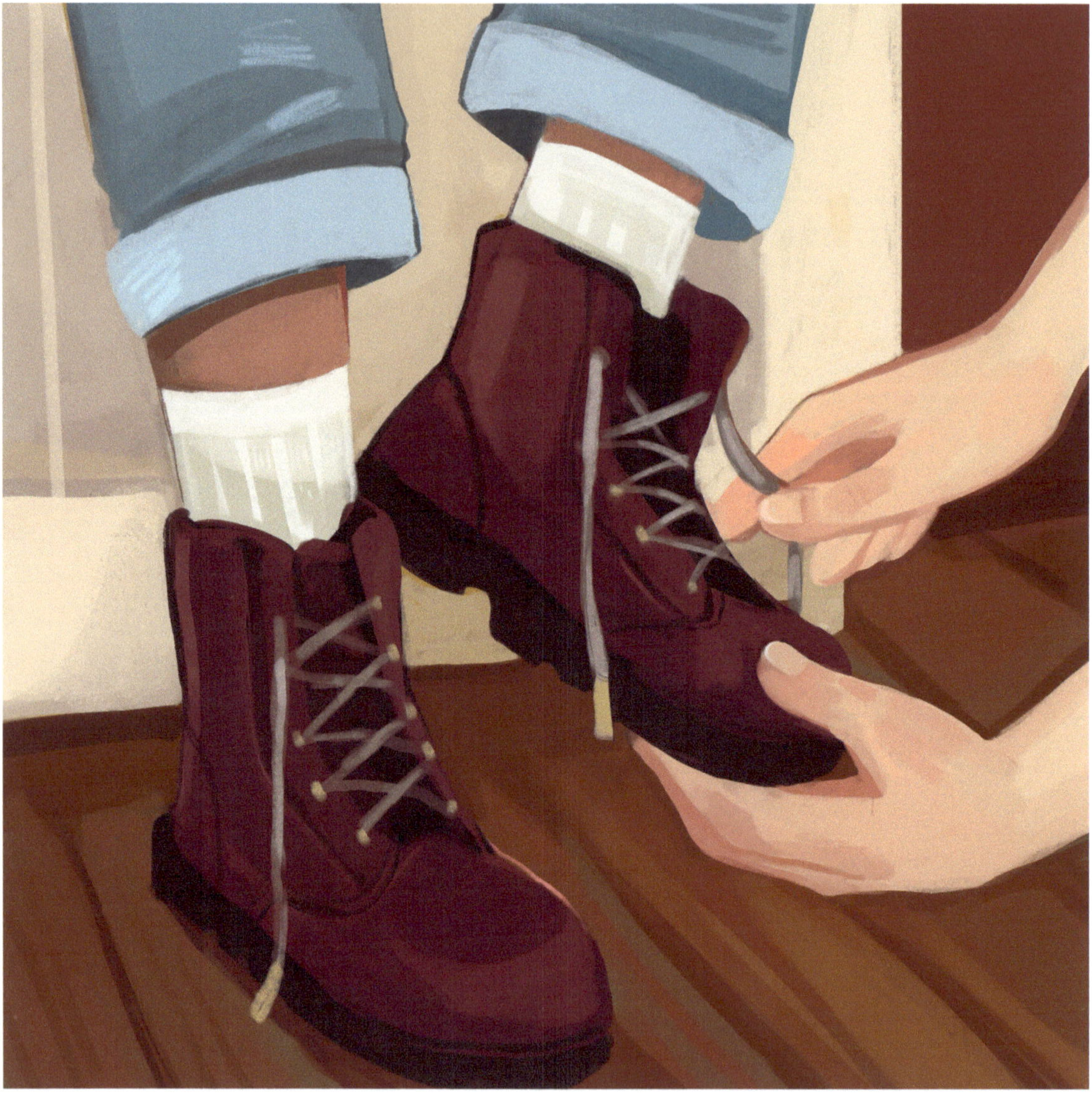

24

Take off their boots

There's nothing like a well-fitting pair of boots—work boots, winter boots, fashion boots, or cowboy ropers. Sometimes it's tough to get them off if they don't have a zipper. If you don't have a boot jack, save your honey some extra grunting and grabbing by offering to slide them off. Remember to anchor yourself so you don't get pulled out of your chair, and pull from the ankle not the toes!

25

Rub their belly

_____

Anyone who has had a stomach ache or indigestion knows
how good it feels to be gently rubbed back and forth, or
maybe in a circle. (It's also good for that time of month
or after big meal, and even better when accompanied
by soothing words.) Make sure to take the time to notice
what is special about the belly button: if it's an innie or an
outie or if it's changed any since the last time you really
looked at it. It's a secret only the two of you will know!

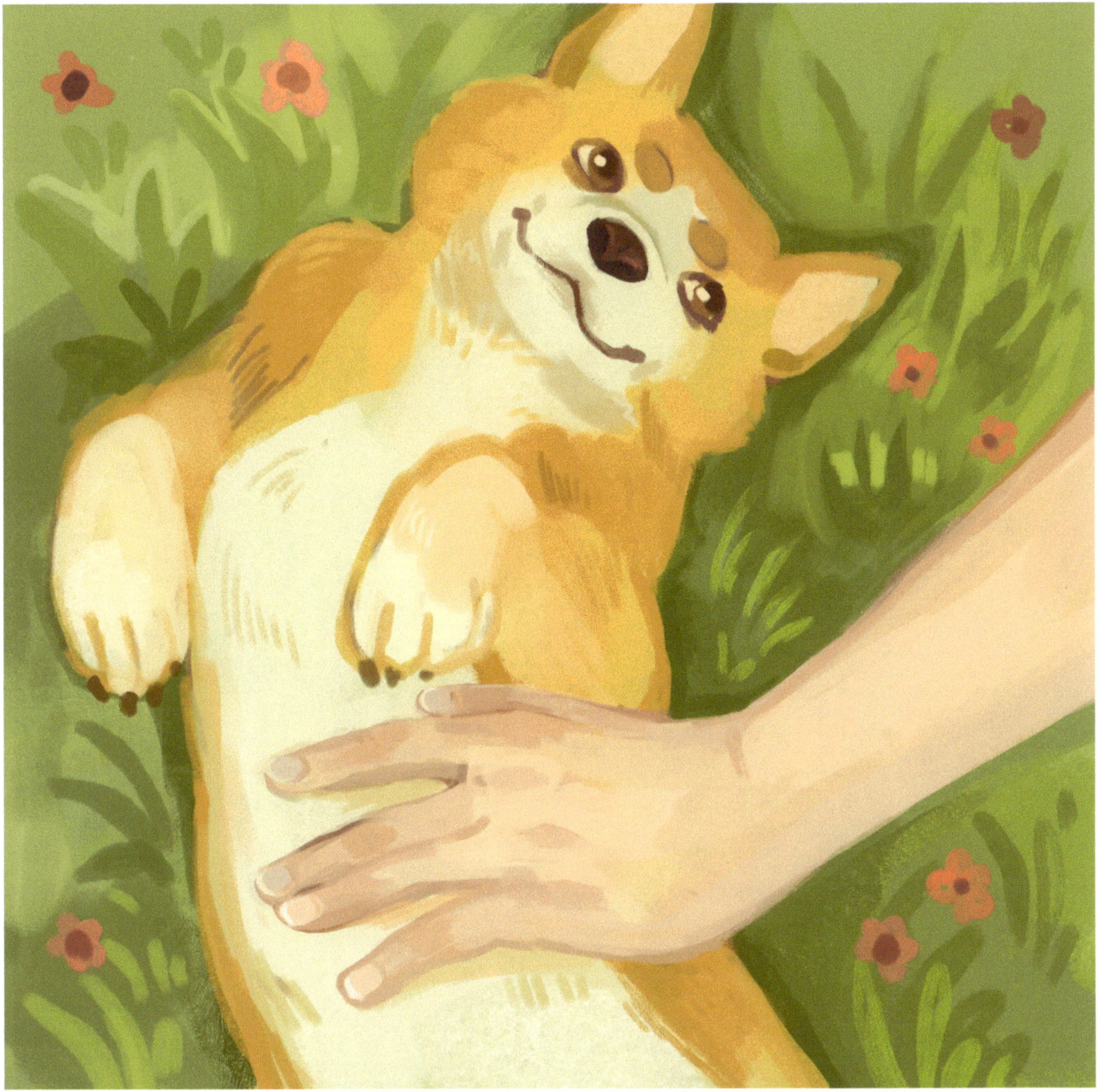

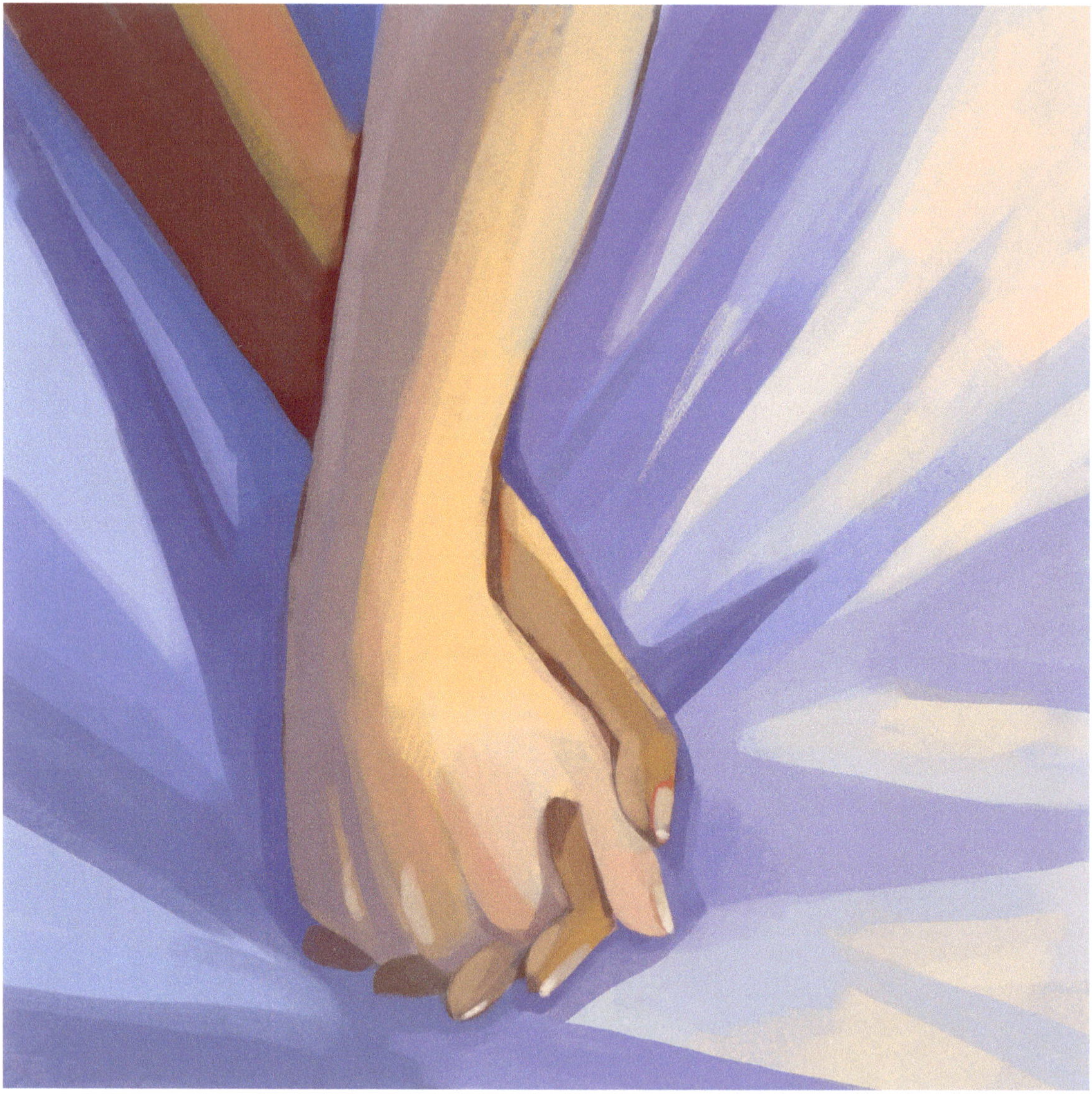

26

Take an afternoon nap

When you sneak away for an afternoon nap, enjoy every second! Drink in the sight, smell, taste and touch of your partner. When is the last time you held hands in bed? That can be the perfect time to just be still. Or, ask them about the favorite part of their day, and LISTEN. It's one of the best gifts you can give to your partner—your undivided attention.

27

Make it smell good

Pick a room and make it smell inviting, delicious! Mist the bedroom with lovely eucalyptus aromatherapy. Light a sea-scented candle in the dining room. Clean the bathroom with a yummy citrus product. Bake bread or cookies in the kitchen. Use a pine plug-in in his Man Cave. It's always nice to come home to a wonderful fragrance—but only do one at a time so you don't induce a headache when they mix!

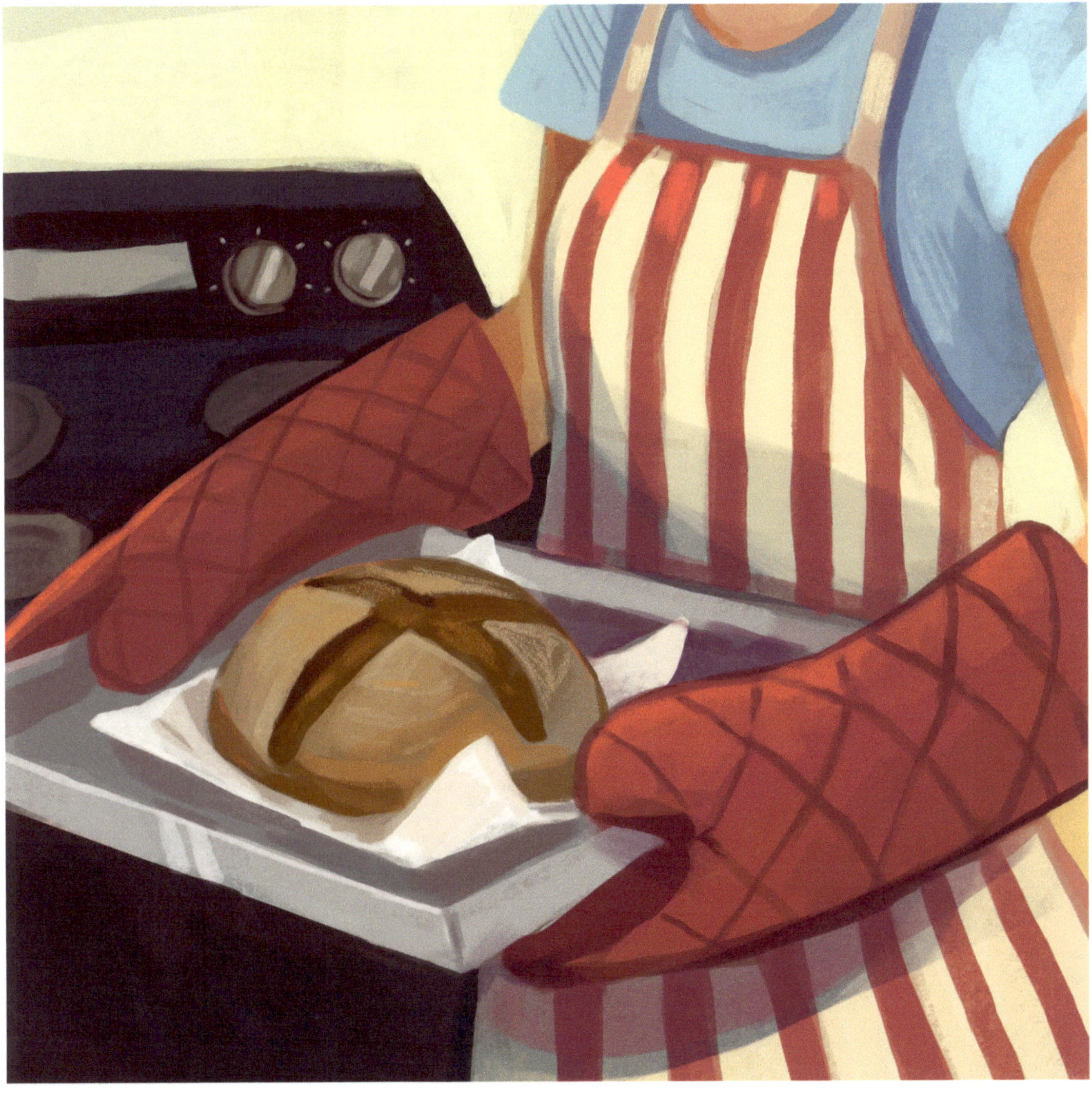

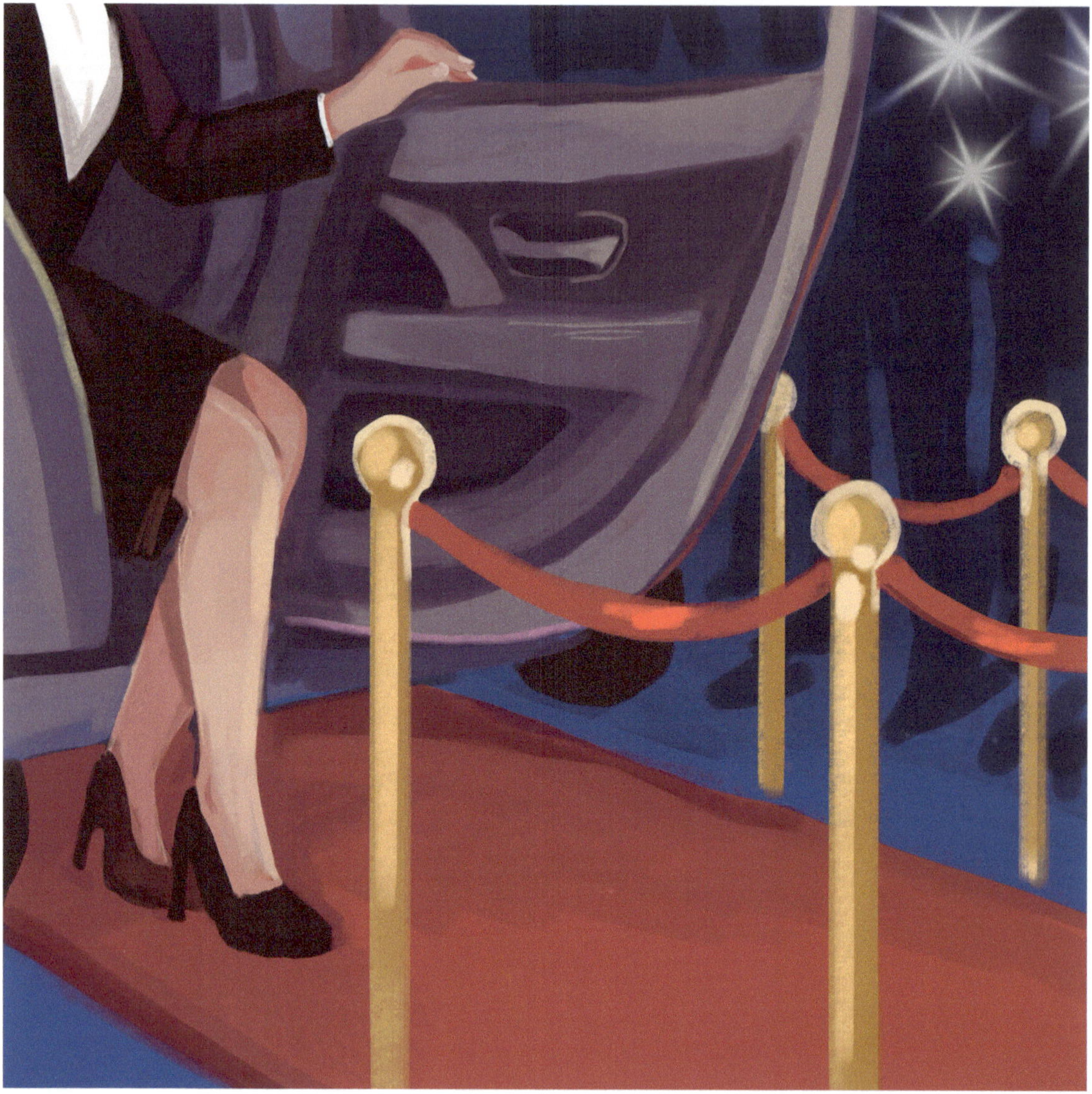

28

Open the car door

You may not have a red carpet to roll out in front of the car door, but you can pretend with some panache! Come out to greet them like a celebrity with a big "Welcome Home!" When your partner is carrying something, anticipate which door they need you to open, or if they need help carrying it, offer. Or, if they're leaving instead of returning, open the door with a flourish. Secure them inside by pulling the seatbelt, and gently closing the door. Leave them with a kiss!

29

Read spiritual insights

Why not share special thoughts before going to bed?
These could be meditations, scripture, inspirations, famous
quotes, or cards that you've received recently. We love
little spiritual quotes. Reading to each other when you're
all tucked in can drum up memories from childhood and
prepare you for a good night's sleep with pleasant dreams.

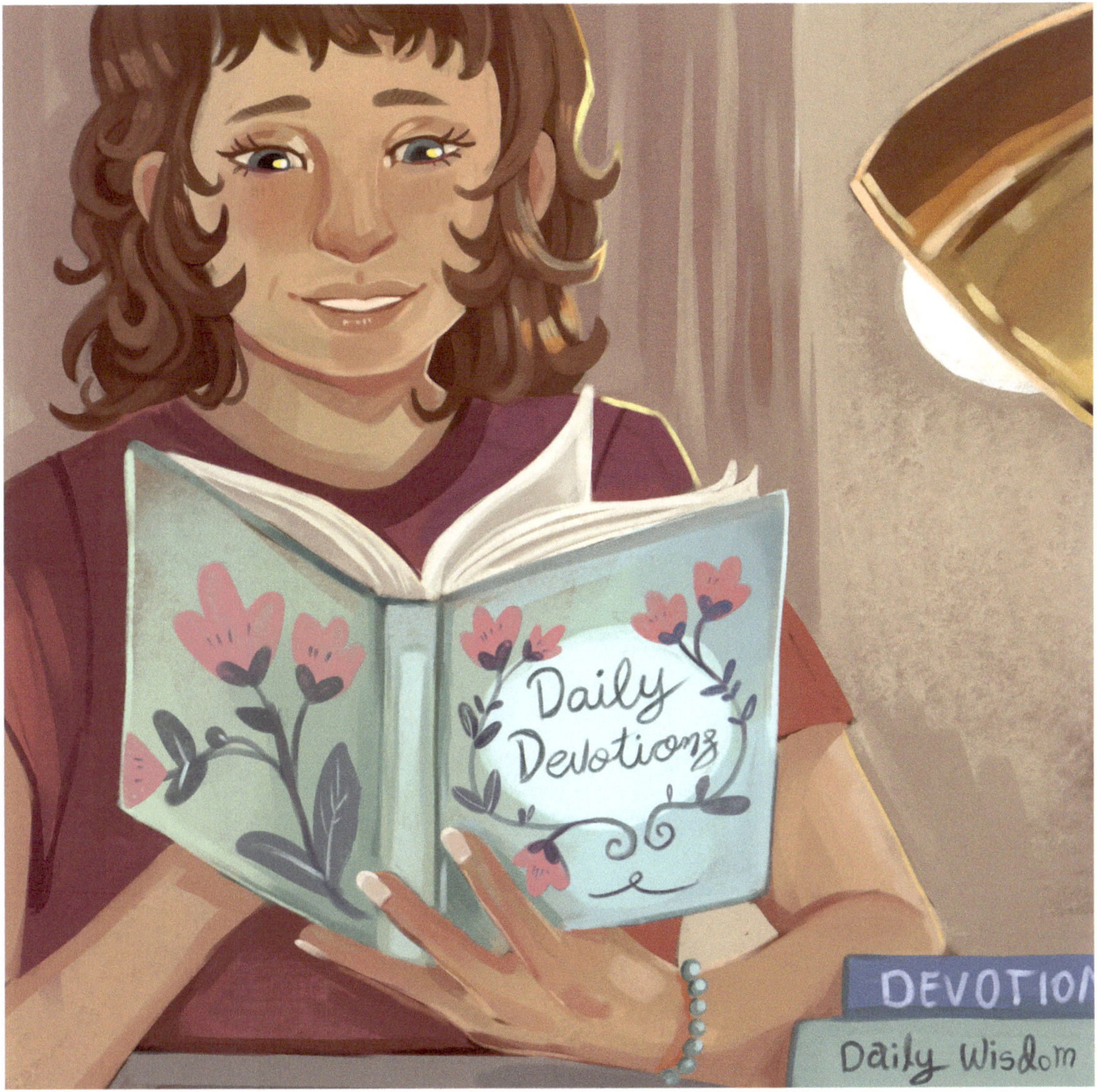
Daily Devotions
DEVOTION
Daily Wisdom

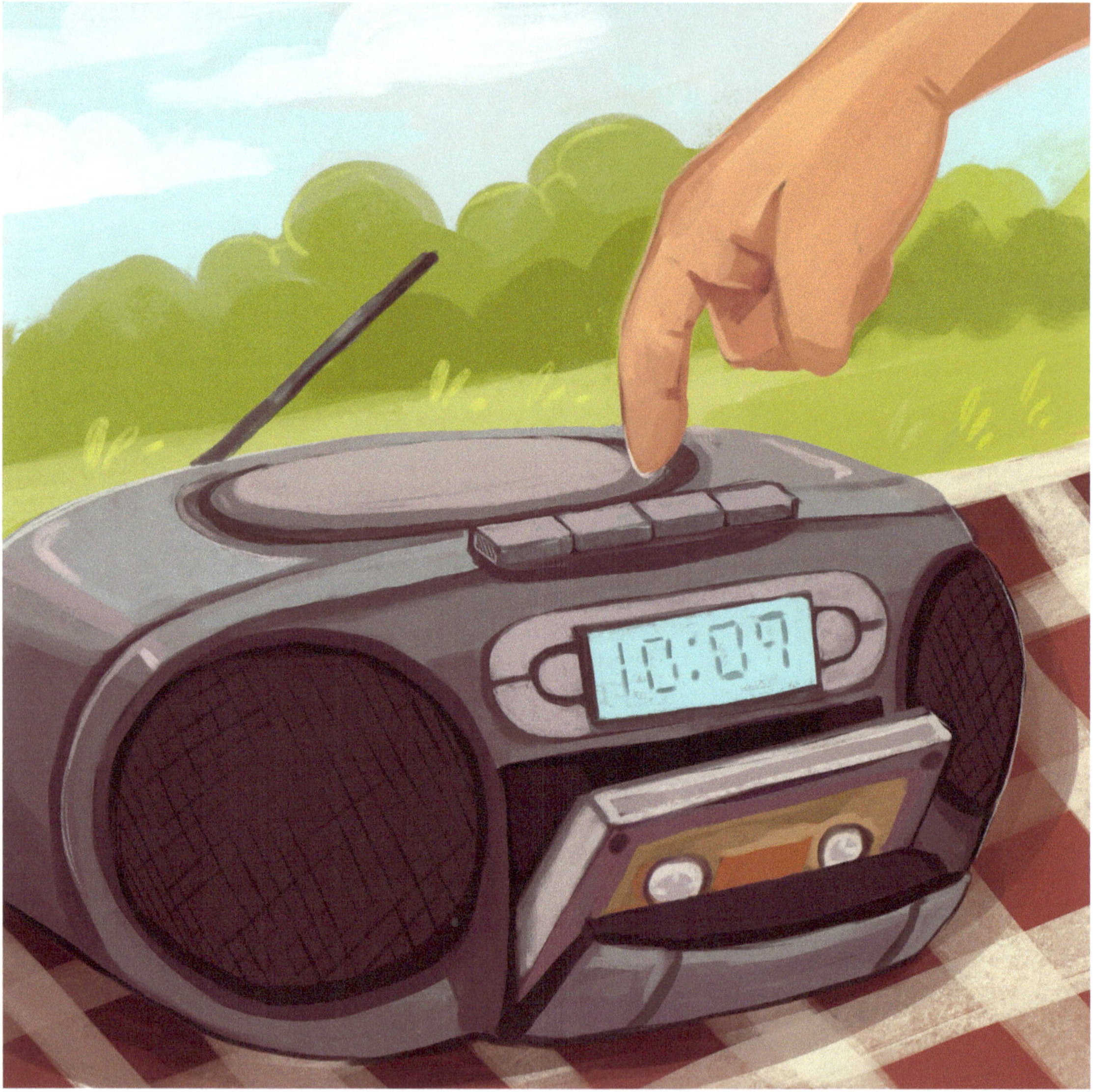
10:09

30

Create your background music

Have you ever thought about movie soundtracks, how they get louder or softer to add to the visual action? How some of the songs are so memorable, like the theme to classics like "The Godfather" or "Dr. Zhivago" or "Twilight"? When you are cooking or relaxing around the house, consider what music to play instead of turning on the TV. Make your own soundtrack to the movie of your life together.

31

Attend important doctor's visits

The "White Coat Syndrome" is well documented: people get nervous in front of medical professionals. When your lovey needs to go, do not let them go alone, particularly if your presence helps to calm them. Pay attention, and take notes to make sure you remember the doctor's comments right. Then, get a phone number or email of someone you can call if you have questions later.

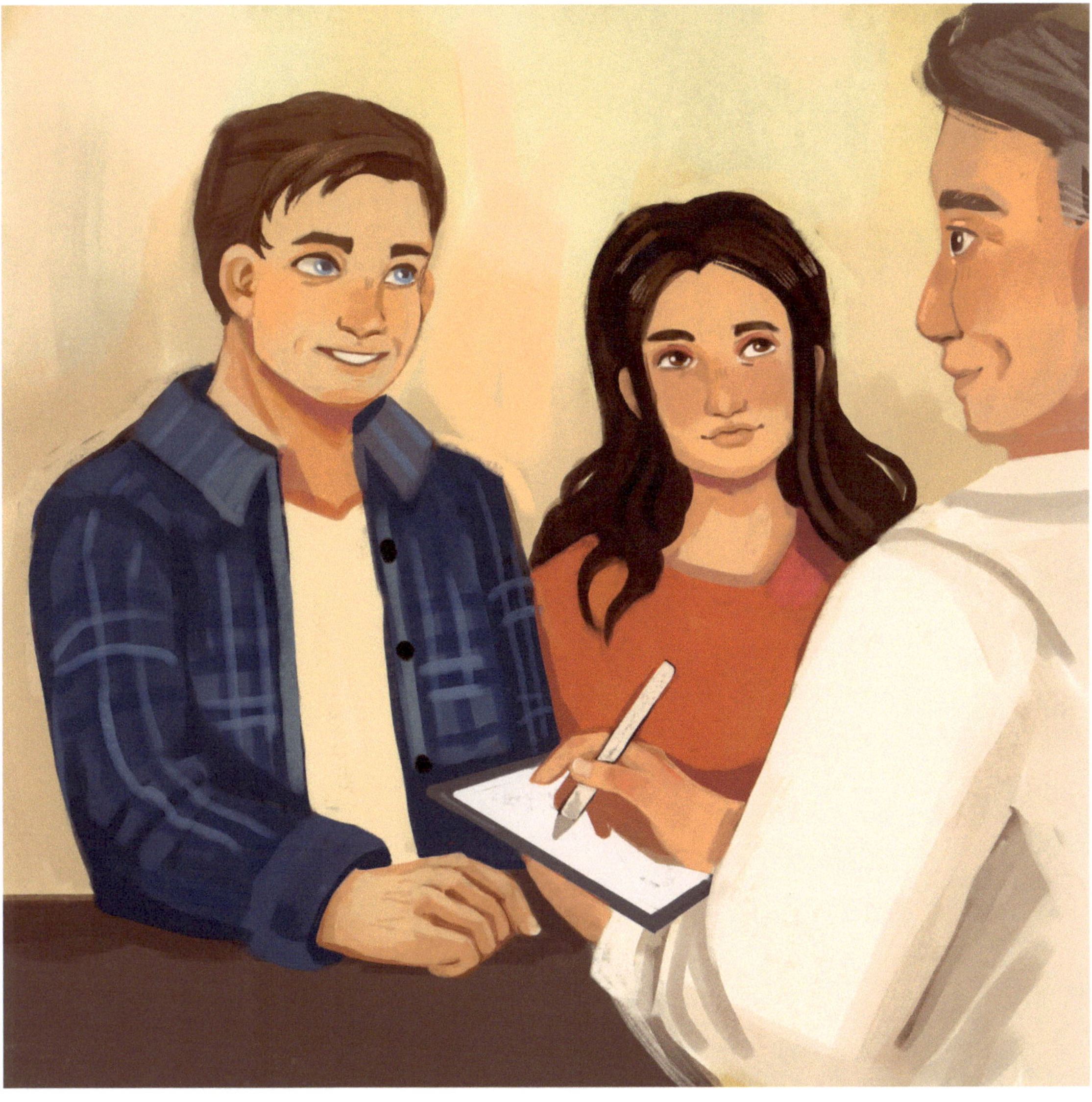

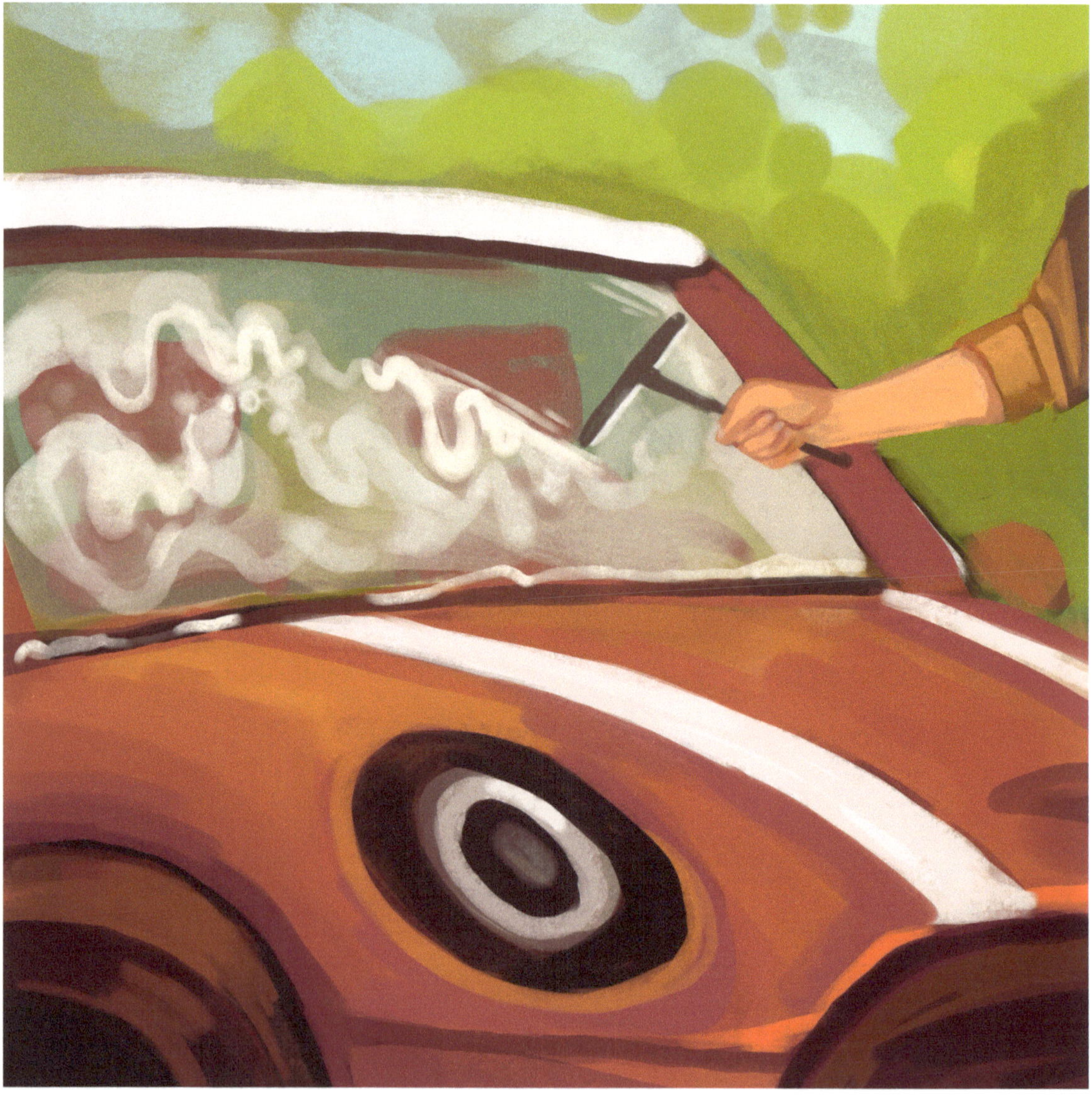

32

Wash their windshield

Car windshields attract bugs. It's just a fact. Cars get dirty. That's a fact too. Unfortunately, they don't wash themselves. When your partner cleans your windshield or your car, it's a pleasure to drive. You can see clearly out the windows, and I'm convinced the car is happier and the ride just feels nicer. It's even better when when your lovey surprises you with the gesture.

33

Make a morning beverage

To start the day off right, prepare and share (when time permits) a cup of tea or coffee, a glass of water with lemon or a sports drink, smoothie, or protein drink. Making a morning routine encourages daily time together in our busy lives. On days when agendas are tight or there is no interest in a full meal, the beverage is a great solution.

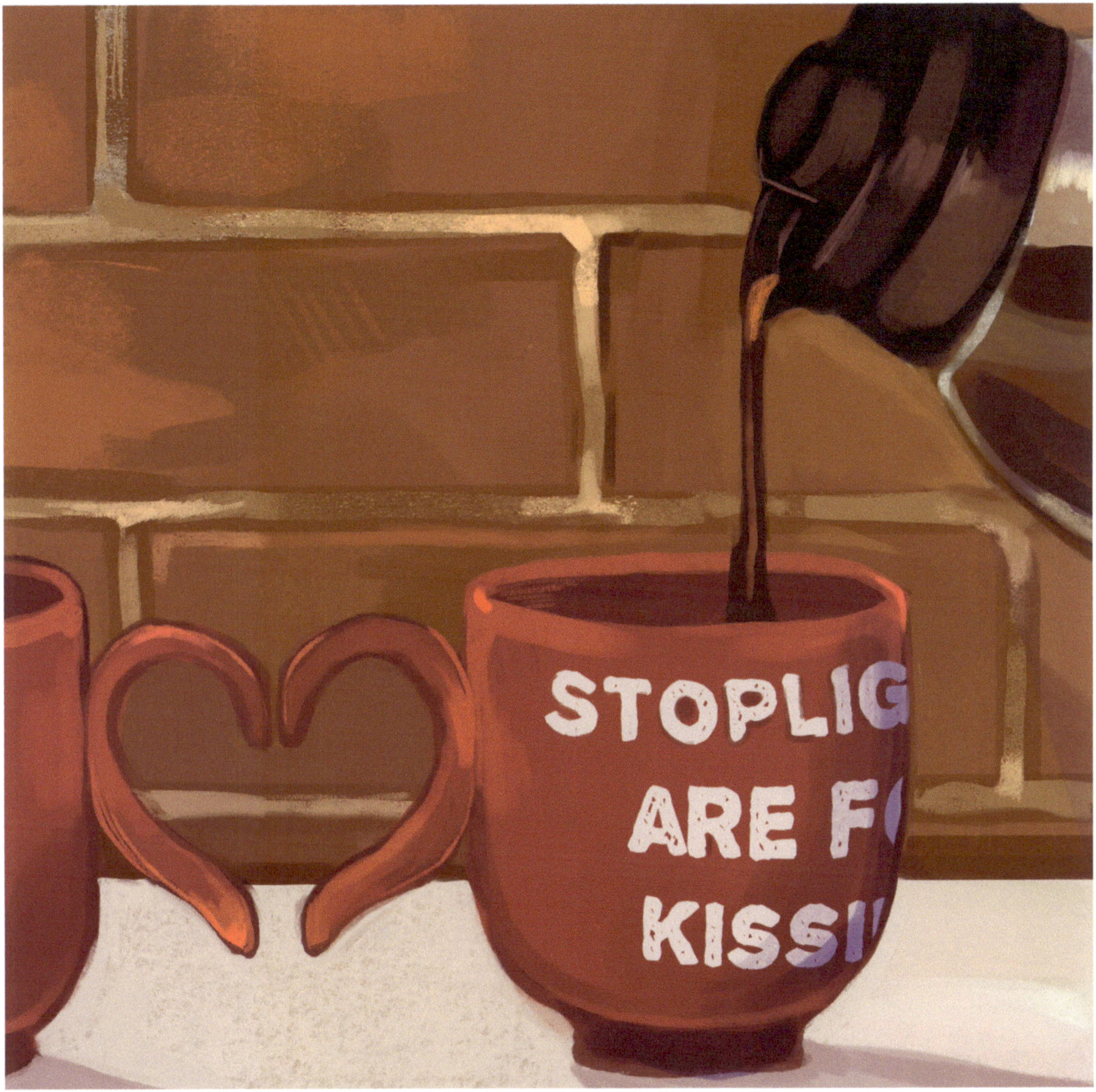
STOPLIG
ARE F
KISSI

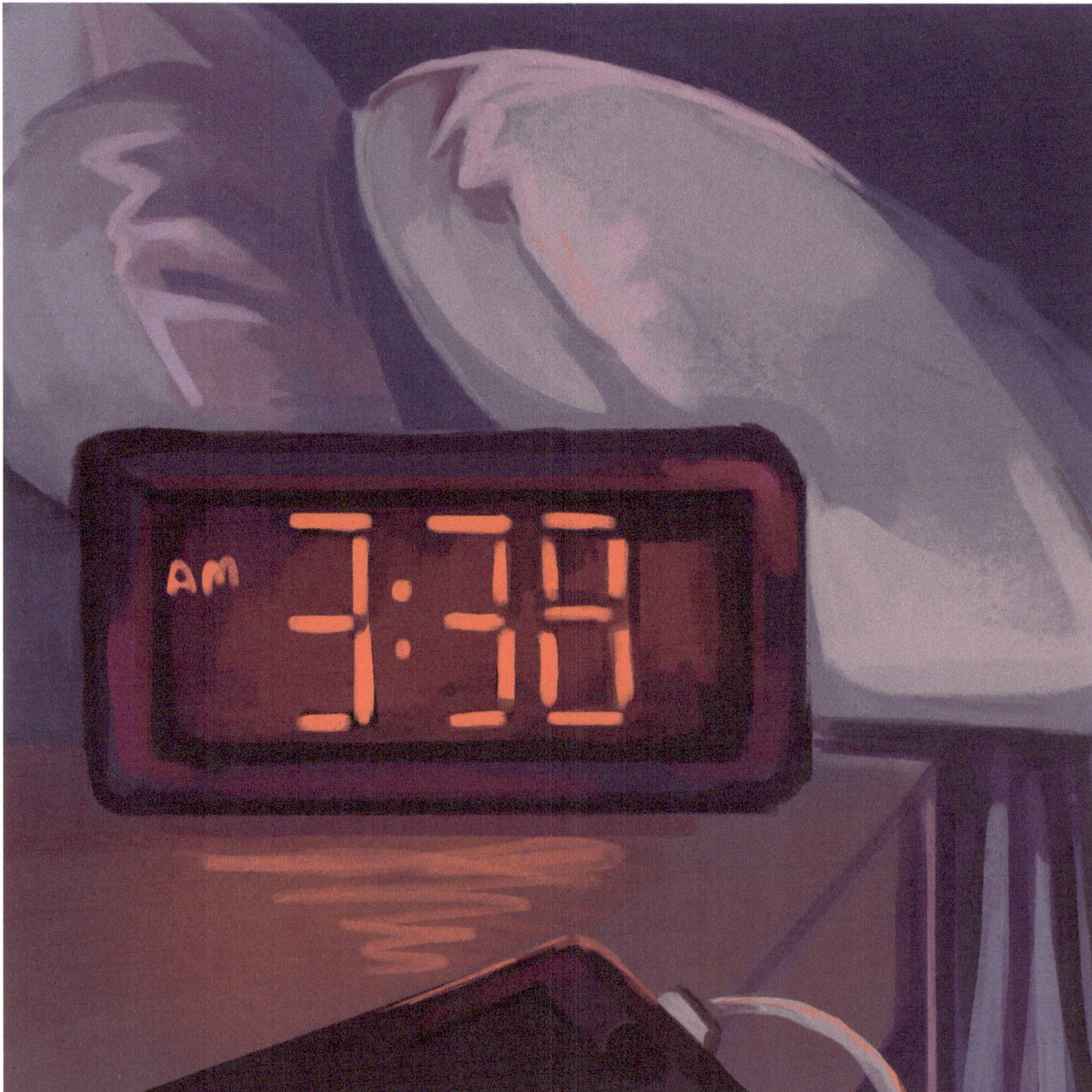
AM
3:38

34

Wake up and listen

If one of us is tossing and turning, it often helps to put us at ease to talk about whatever is upsetting or making us nervous. Although we may be tired in the morning, it's a wonderful way of connecting and including each other in what is exciting, worrisome, or complex. We value each other's contributions, even if our perspectives are different. We often solve problems or generate new ideas together in the middle of the night—two minds are better than one.

35

Care for their shoes

When I was a very small girl, I saw my father shine his shoes for the first time. As with many of his generation, he learned to do it in the military, and kept doing as a habit. The weather-proofing and polishing efforts looked good and assisted in making his favorites last longer. Not all of our footwear needs to be shined, though. As an alternative, consider cleaning your loved one's boots or shoes after gardening, hiking, or walking. It will get them ready for the next adventure or for storing off-season.

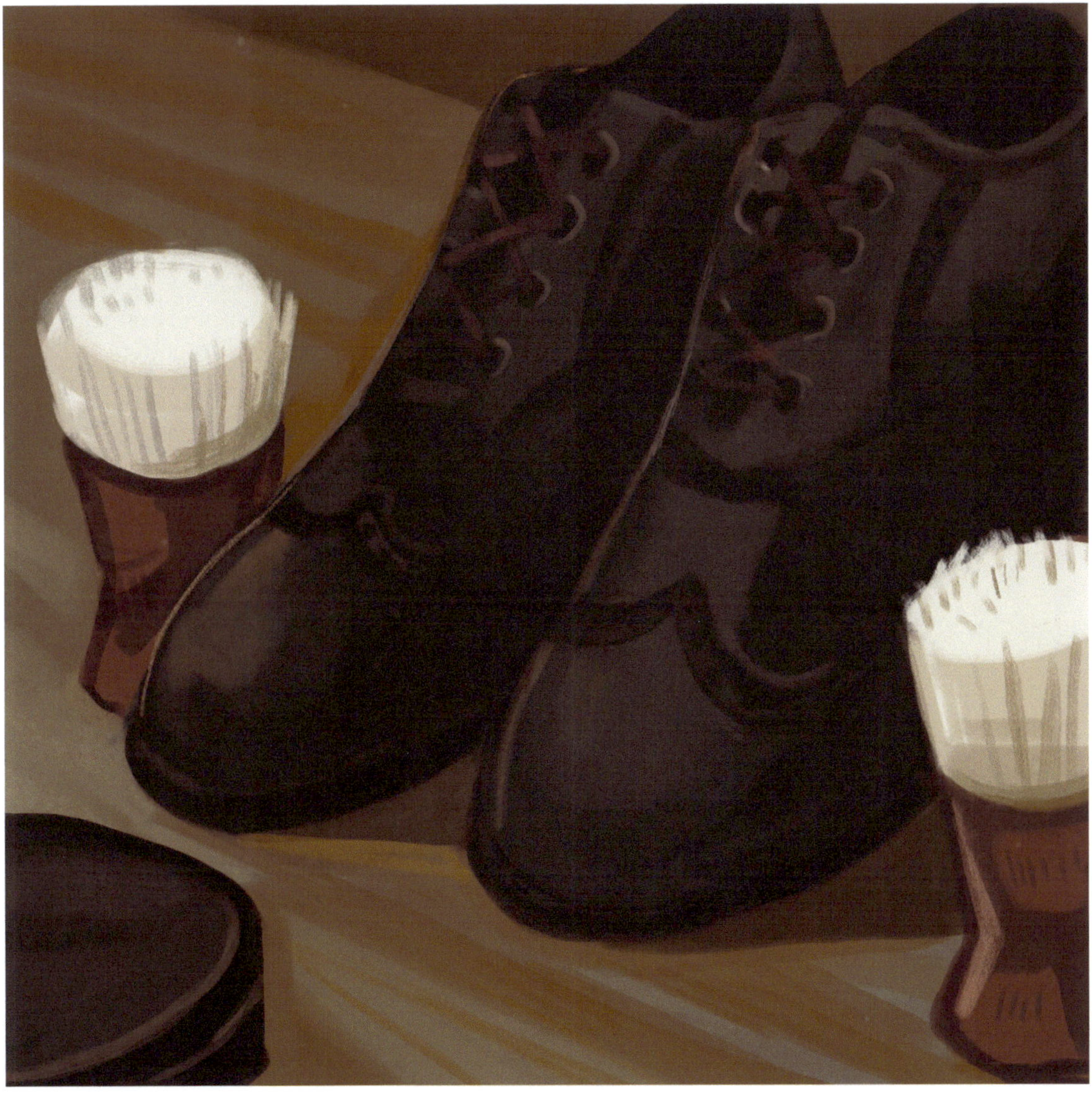

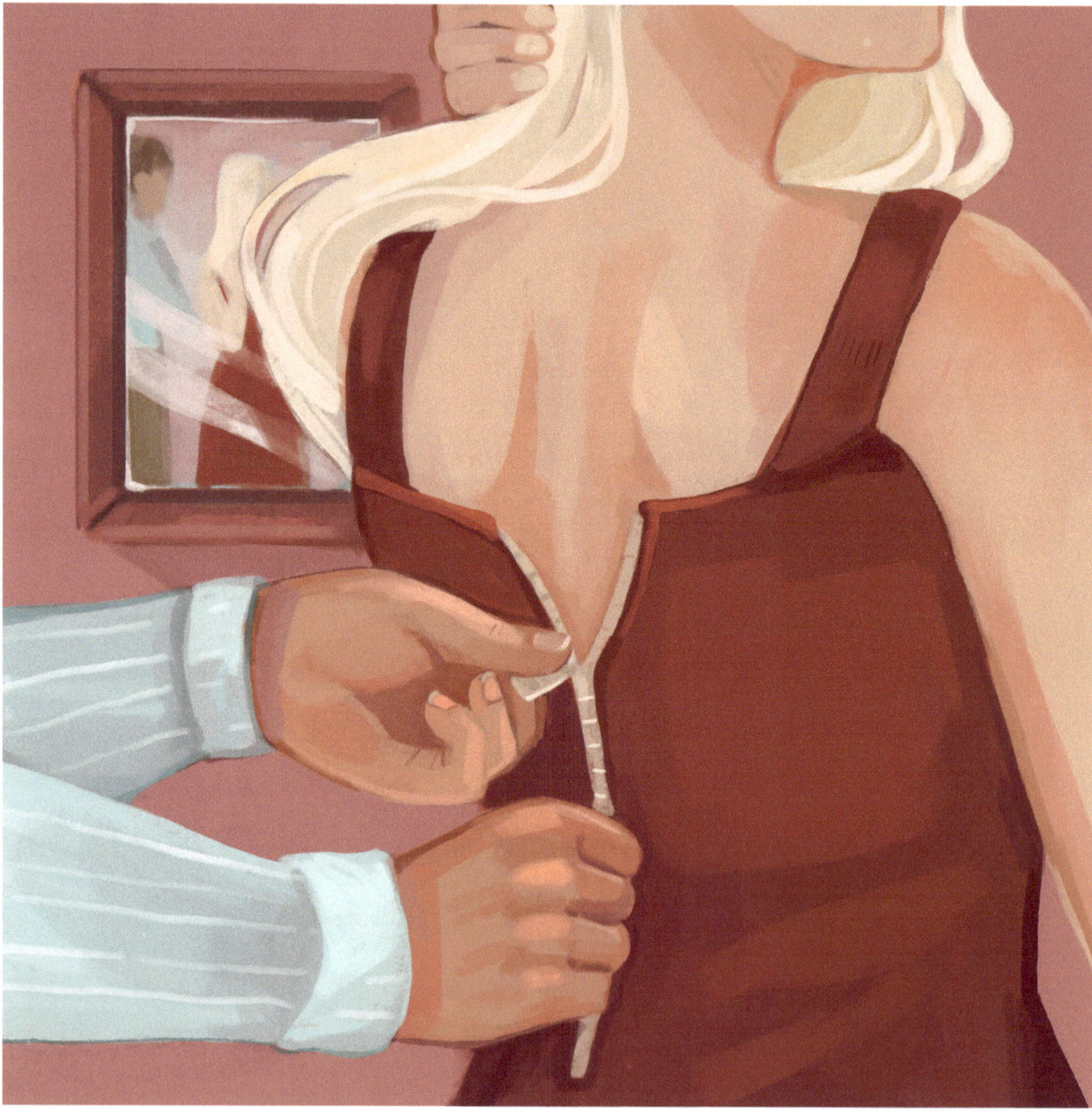

36

Fasten up

At a recent conference, a friend of mine was in the hotel elevator when a very attractive woman got in and asked him to finish zipping up her dress. She couldn't reach it and didn't know who else to ask. He did, and he saw her at their meeting later. She thanked him with a smile. When you've got a hard-to-reach hook, zipper or button, your partner can be a godsend. Ask for aid on those little challenges to be sure you look your best and avoid a wardrobe malfunction.

37

Pump up their bike tires

Riding bicycles can be fun for people of all ages! Whether you ride together or they go alone, servicing their bicycle is a loving way to show you care about their safety. Pump up their tires, wipe down their frames if they're muddy, oil the chain, or get the bike to the shop. A little thing like that will put a smile on them as they ride safely.

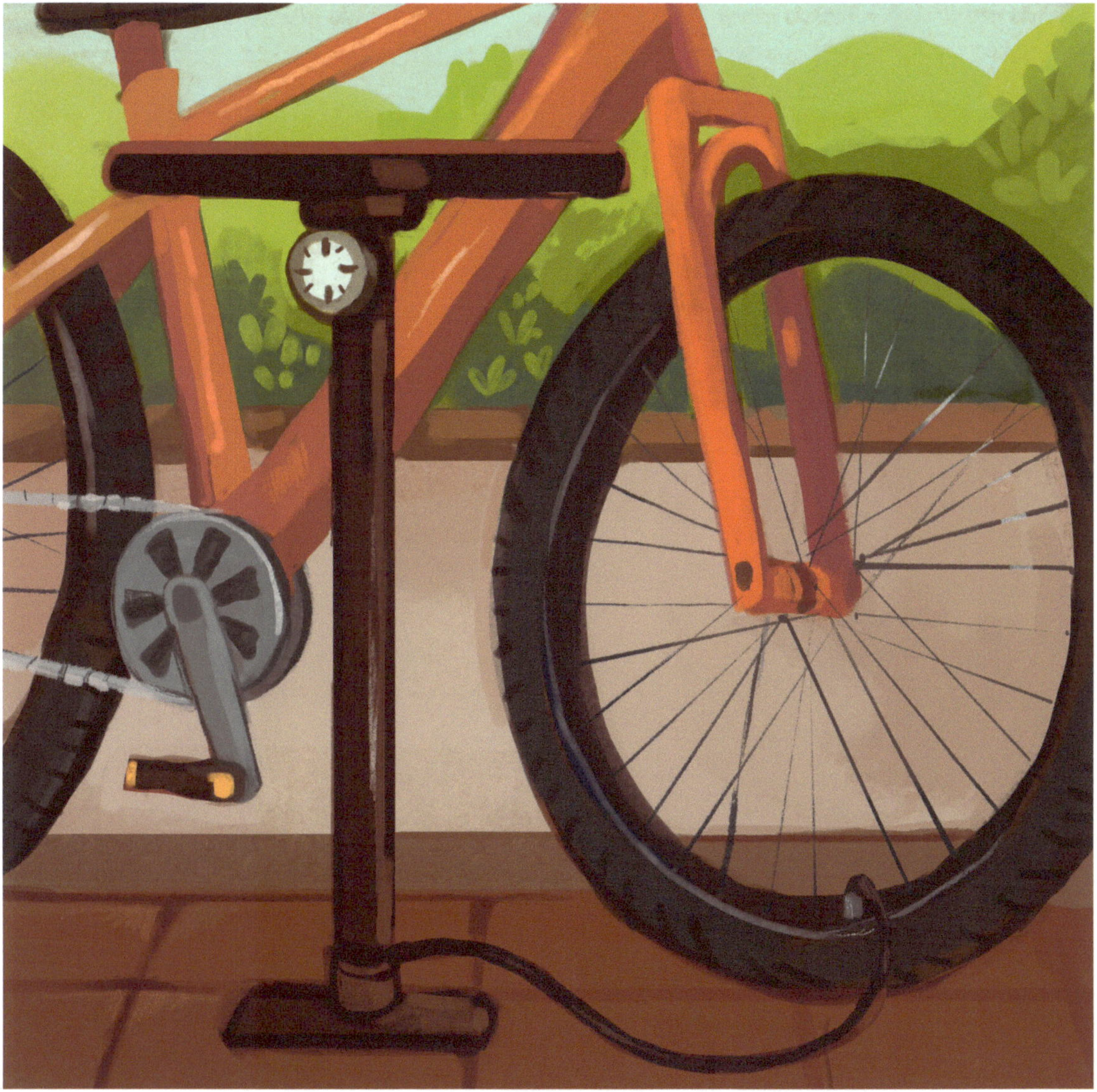

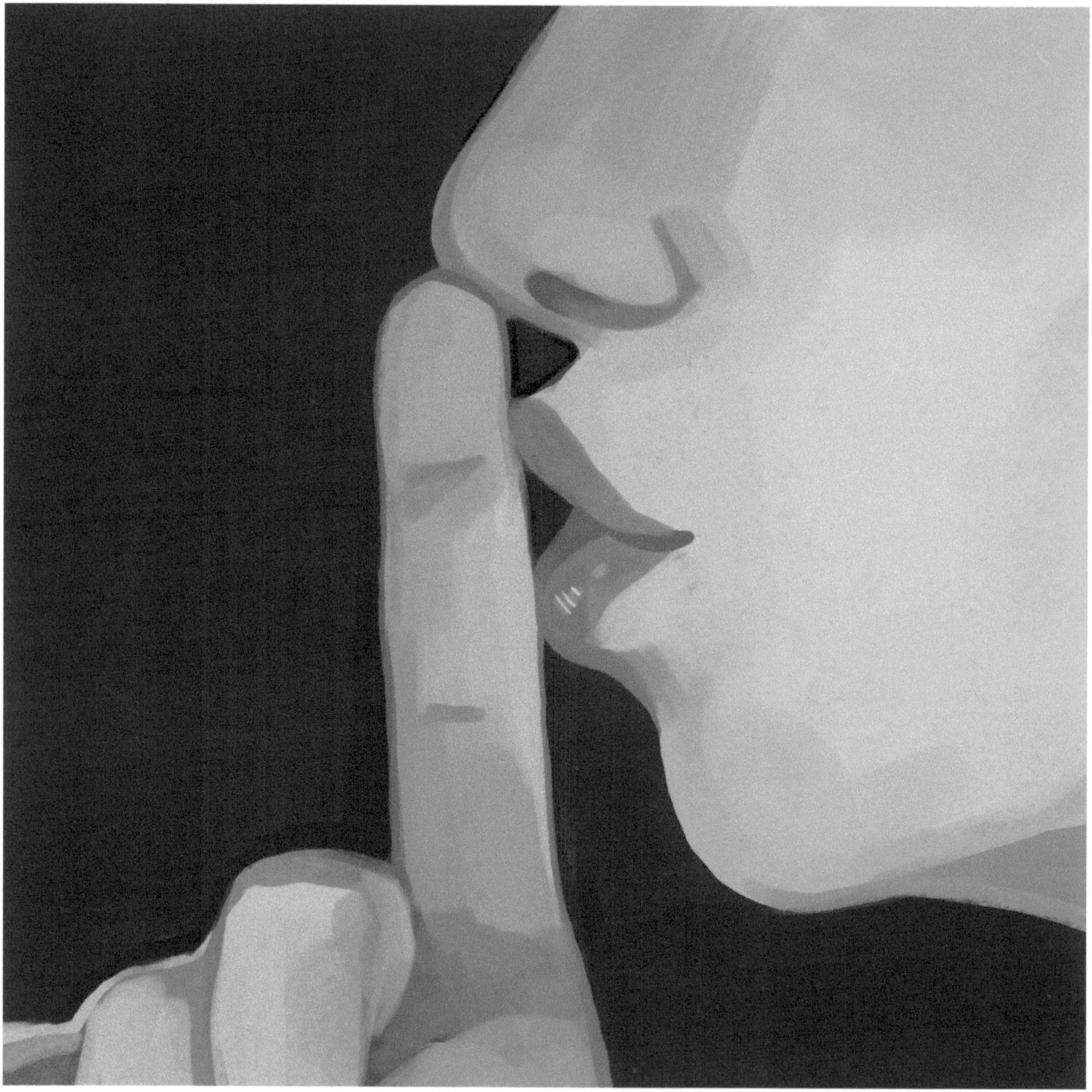

38

Share private gestures

Some couples I know have secret gestures and words they use for more efficient communication. Like playing with an ear when it's time to go, offering an elbow for holding onto, or giving a certain smile or wink to say "You Are The Best!" or "I'm Proud of You!" You may also try a finger to lips with anticipation of private time, like "No excuses, the dishes can wait!" Enough said.

39

Clean a closet or drawer together

Organizing a dresser or bureau can be a daunting task, especially if you change out winter clothes for summer ones or vice versa. Working with your partner makes it easier— they can give you opinions about what looks good on you or what is past its prime. Together you can decide what to donate to Goodwill or The Salvation Army, friends, or kids. Then, you can have another adventure giving it away.

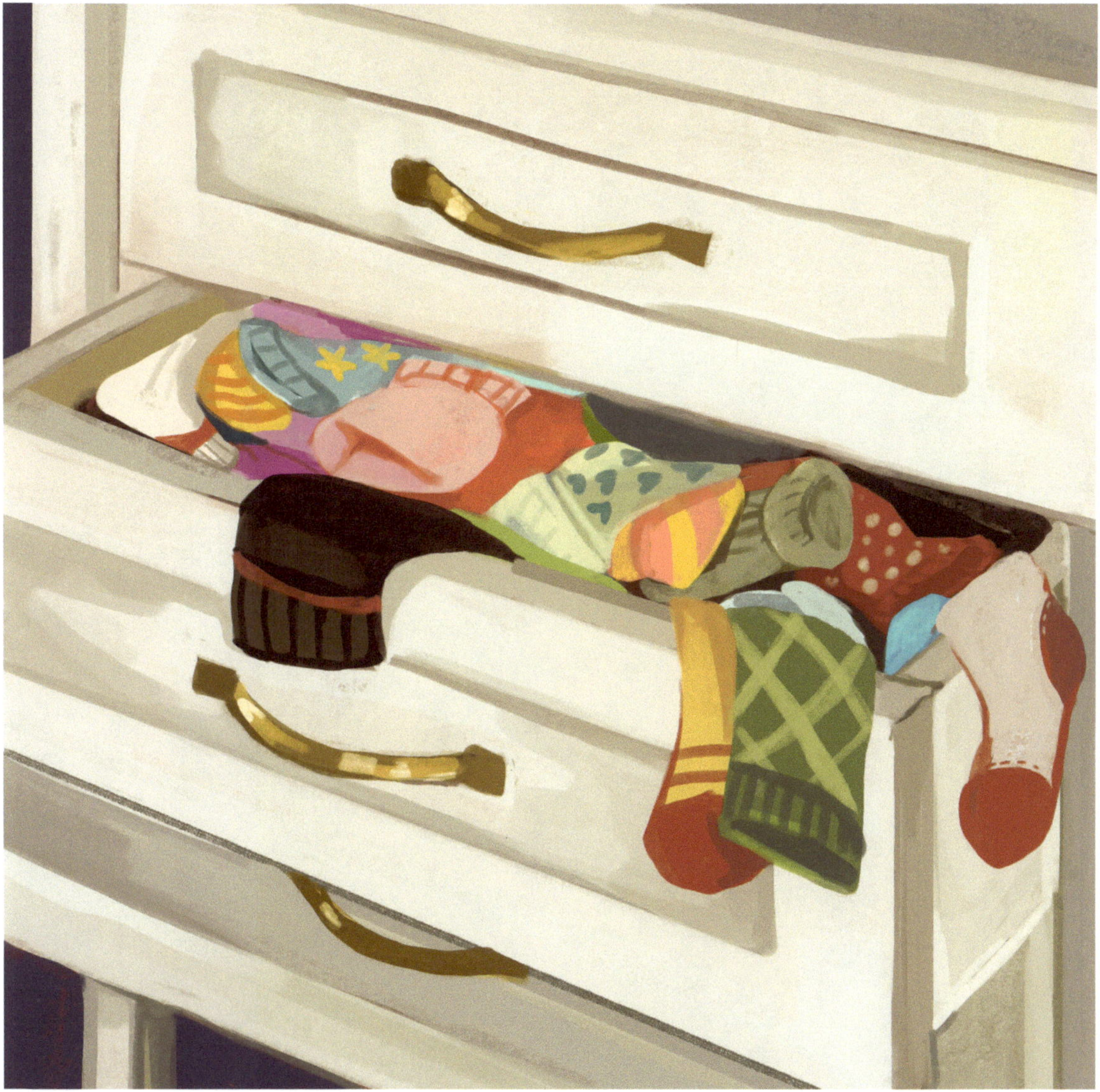

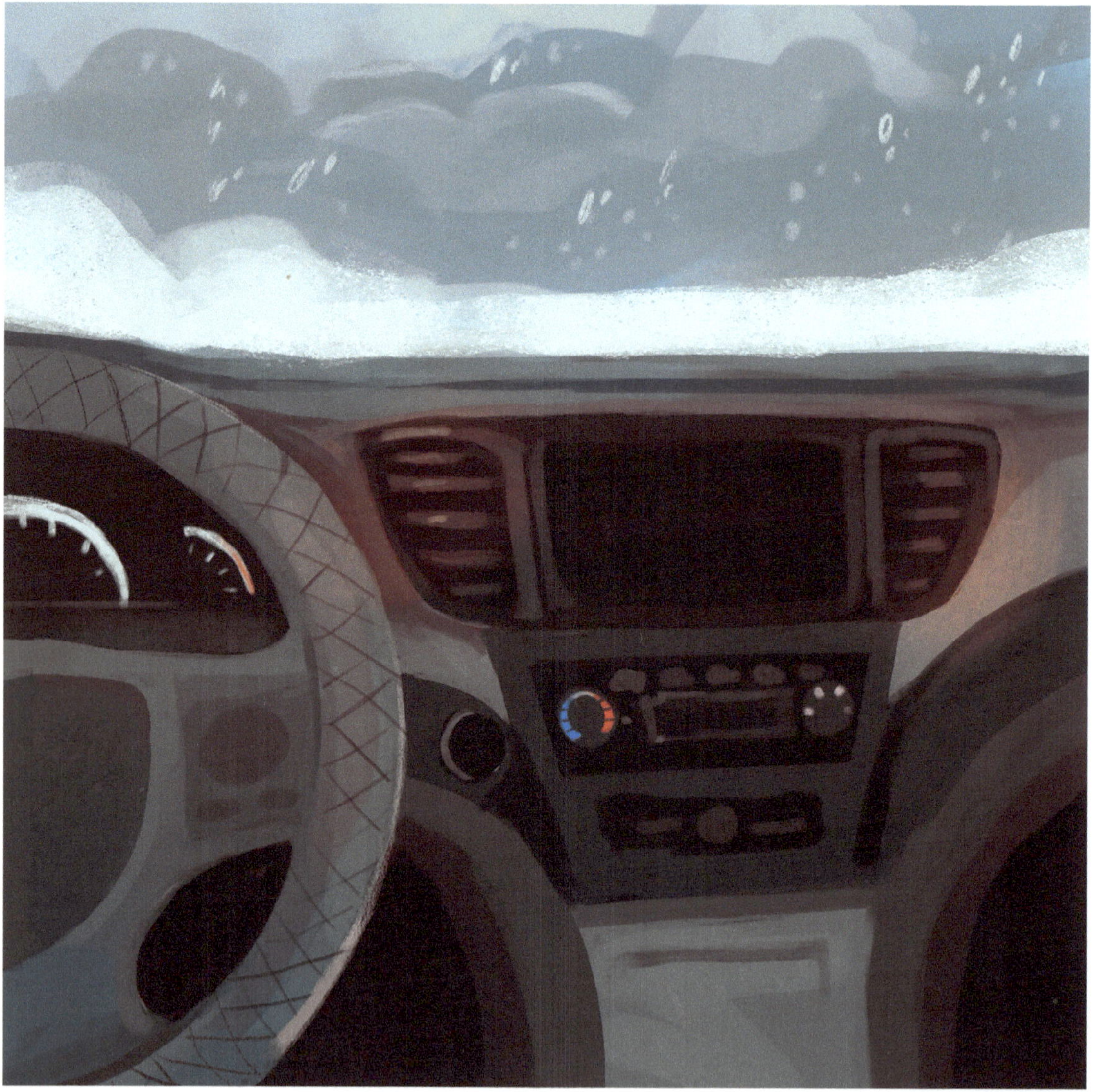

40

Prep their ride

We all know how busy our days can be, but sometimes if you're working from home, you can get the car ready for your honey to drive. In the cold, start the car and then turn the heater on to warm it up. De-ice the windows while you're at it! When it's warm, start the car and roll down the windows or crank the AC. It's a caring way to get their journey started on a good note.

41

Manage the pet food or litter box

We love our furry family members. However, it may become a little bit of a chore to manage the pet food, address the pet messes, or clean the litter box. Not to mention, how to train or when to visit the vet. Strategizing with your partner on these tasks—like where and how to put out the food—can make it easier to love your pet together, as you share their care.

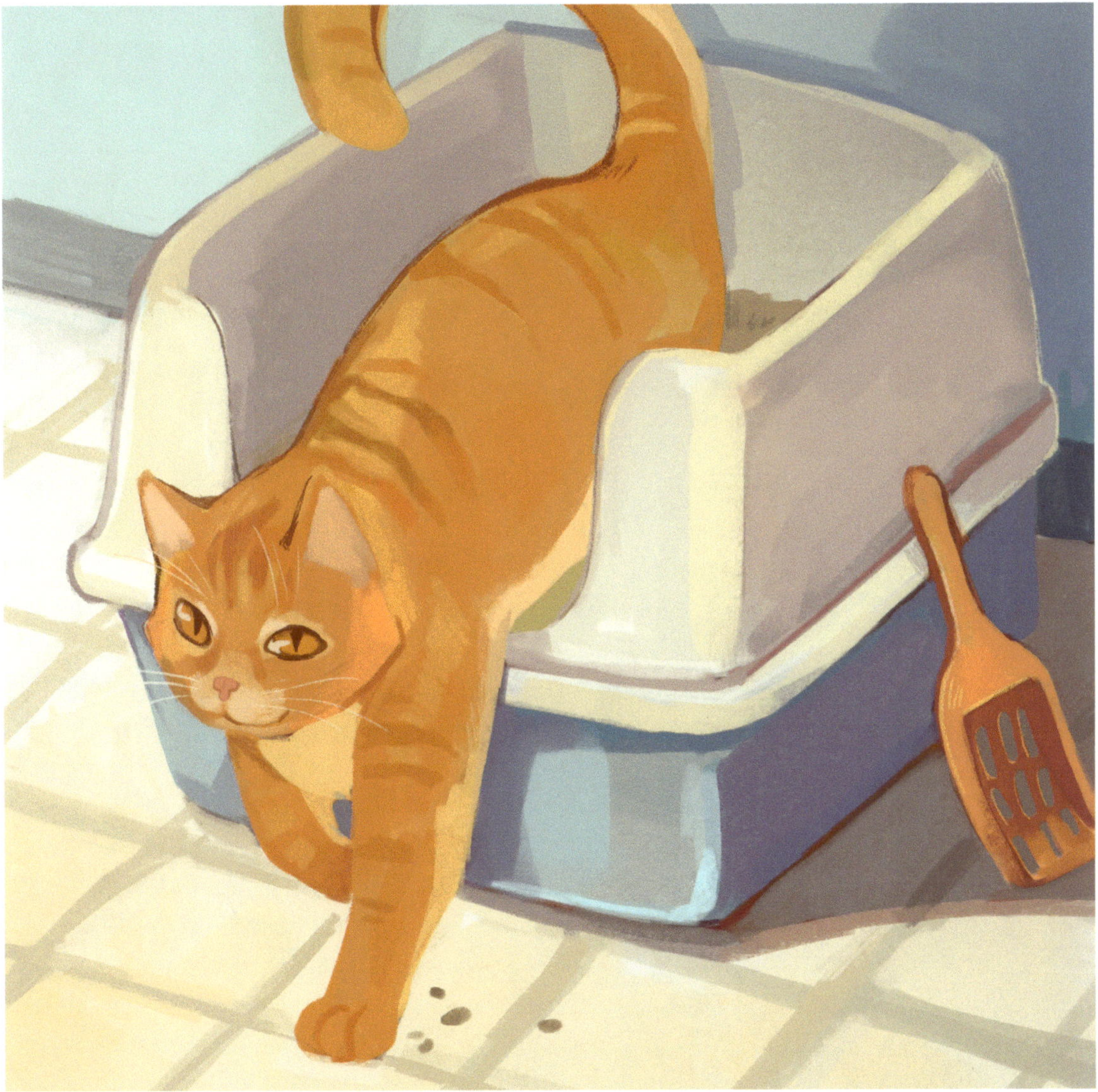

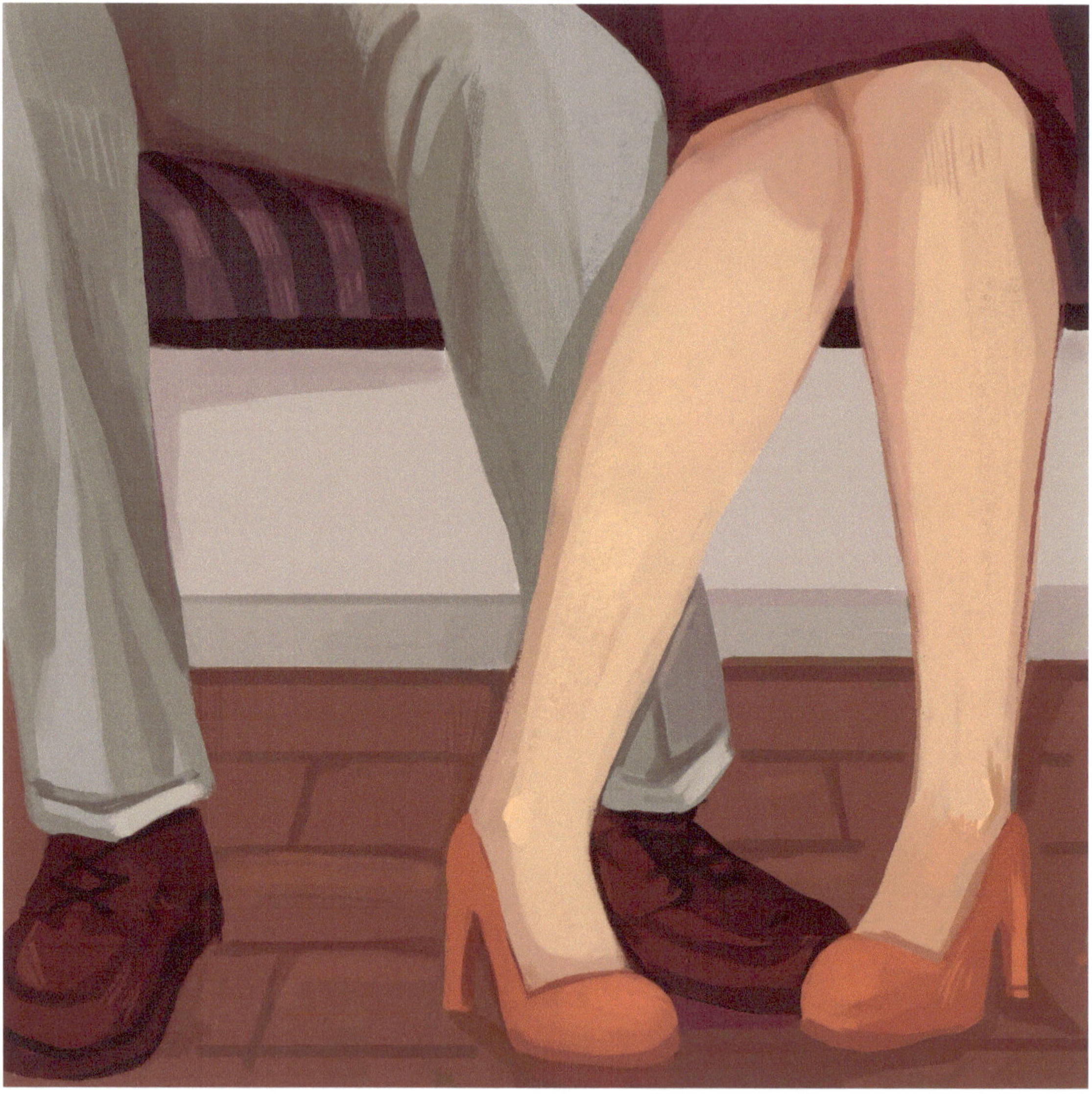

42

Play "Footsies"

When you're on the couch watching TV, in restaurants,
outdoors at a picnic, or at the beach, you've got the
opportunity to reach for your partner with your foot or shin.
We love to do this at casual dinner spots when we're seated
far across from each other. It feels like we're connected,
even though we may not be able to hear each other well.

43

Match your
socks or t-shirts

When you're children, it may not be as fun to dress alike as it is when you're adults! We have buffalo-plaid fleece lined socks with stop treads—a little silly to have on but the warmest things I own! We wear them on the coldest of nights. On the warmest of days, we sometimes sport t-shirts with logos of his alma mater or mine. Nothing better than having a loving spouse to help cheer your team on to victory!

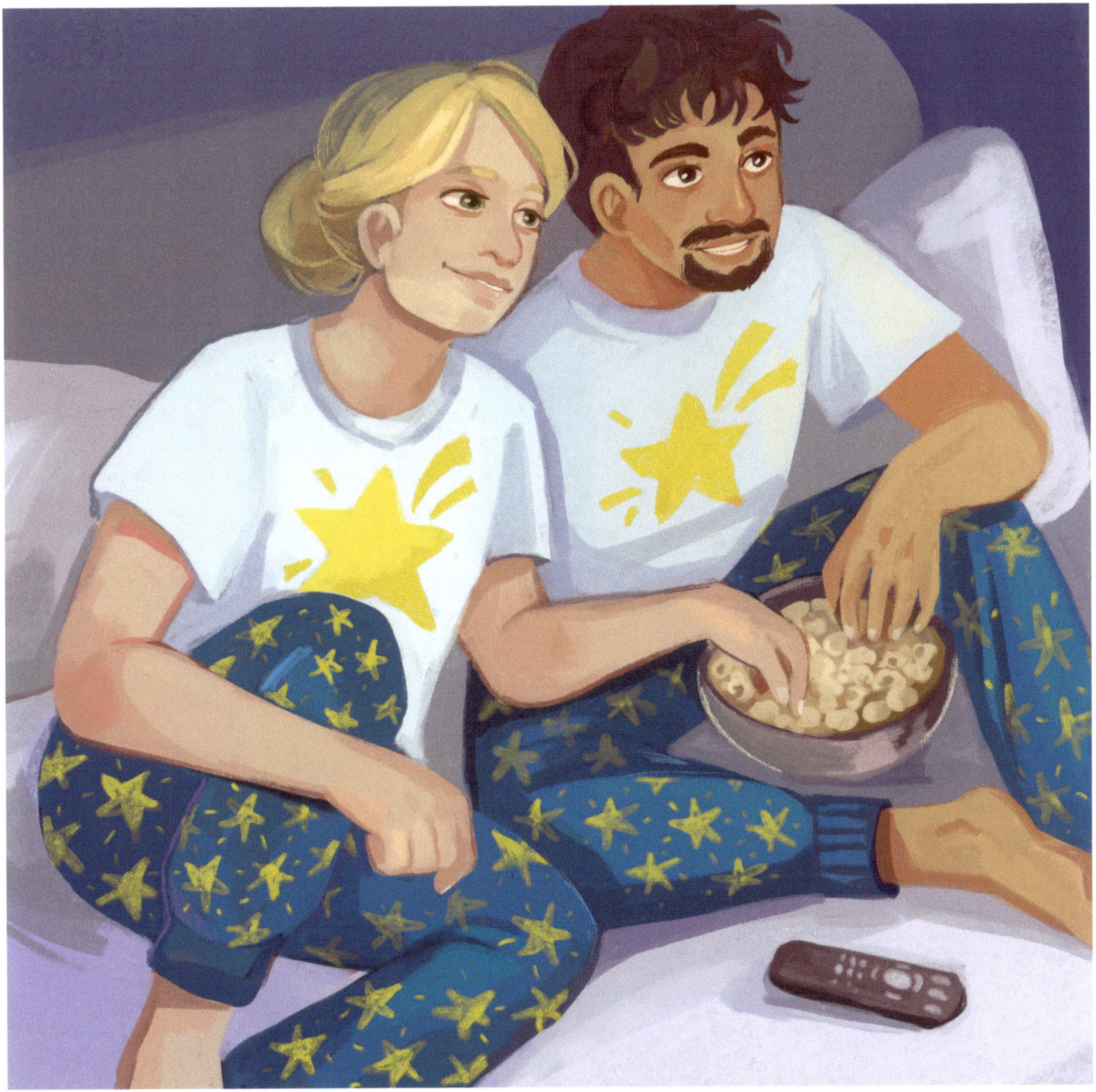

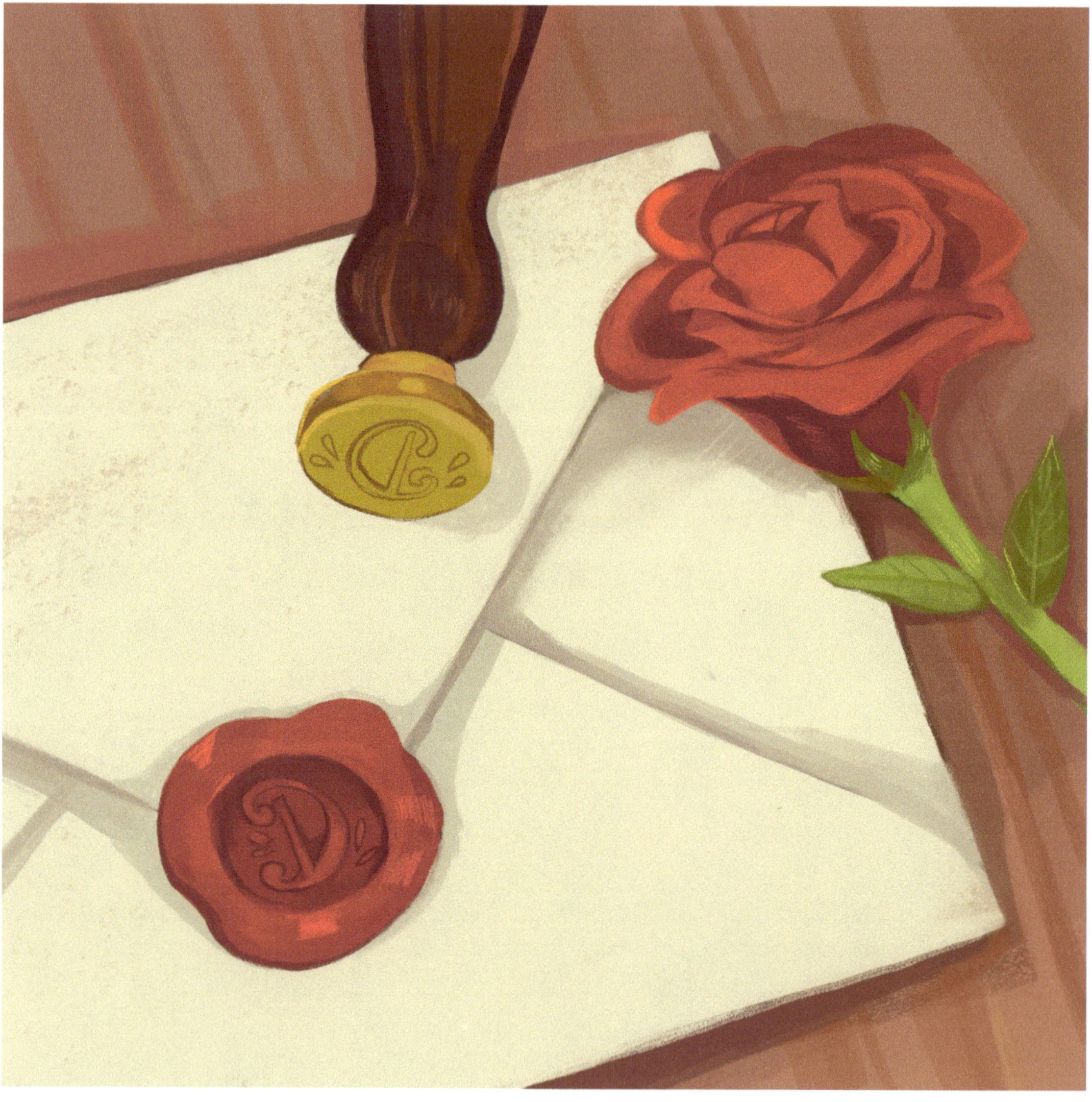

44

Mail a love letter or card

A tradition older than Shakespeare—this act of love has stayed around because it works. It doesn't have to be fancy, just hand-written and left for a surprise discovery. Little wax seals and stamps can be found at a craft store or art supply shop. It takes a little effort, but it's an intimate alternative to the quick DM or email, and one that lasts longer. Your partner may just keep it forever!

45

Hold the ladder or stepstool

Don't you feel so much more secure when someone is holding the ladder or stepstool? One or two steps aren't as scary as three, four or more! For safety, support, and collaboration, hold your partner's ladder. If you're able to assist by handing them a tool, cloth, or batteries for holiday lights, it will certainly not go unnoticed, and may be rewarded later with a hug or kiss!

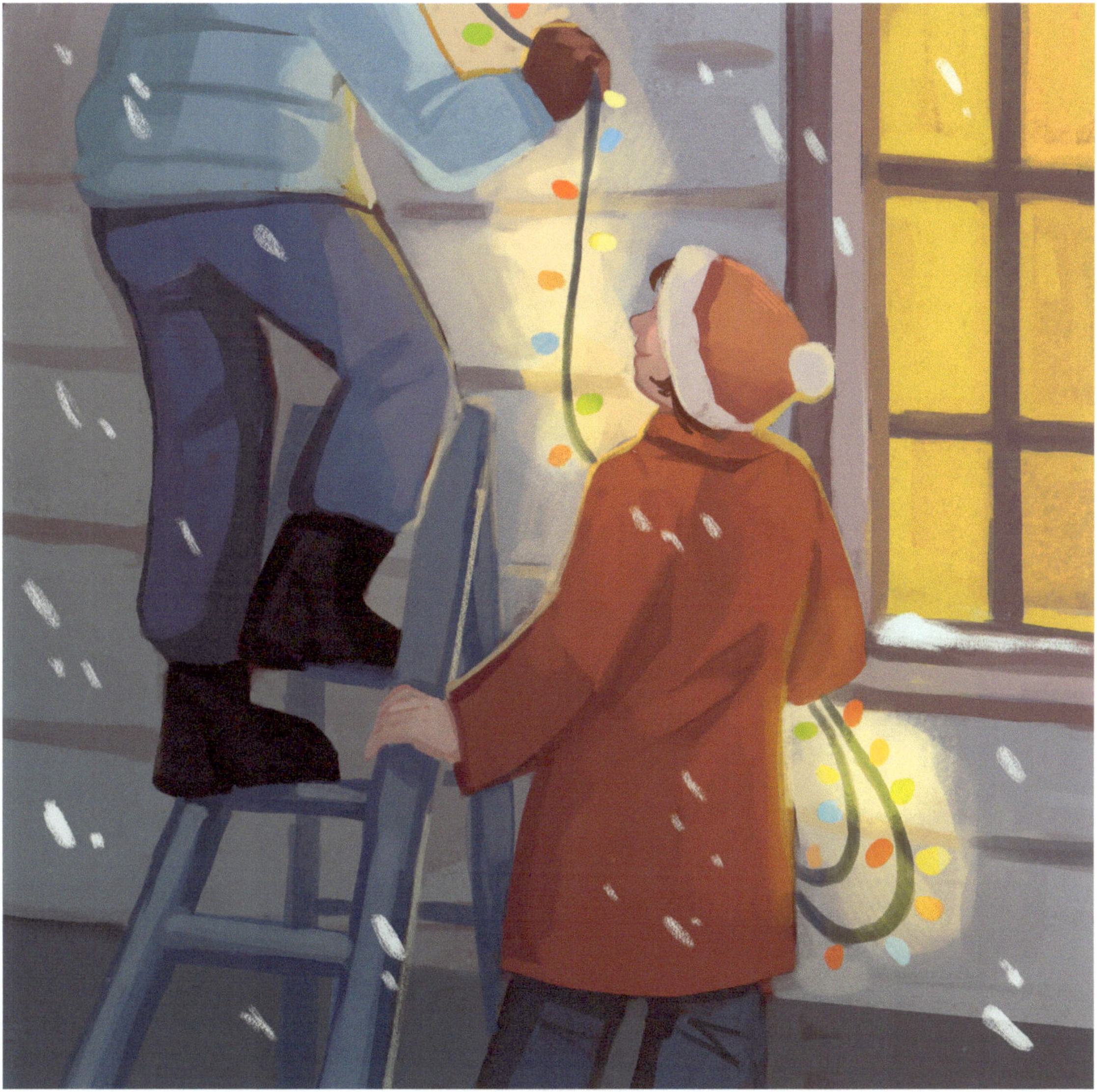

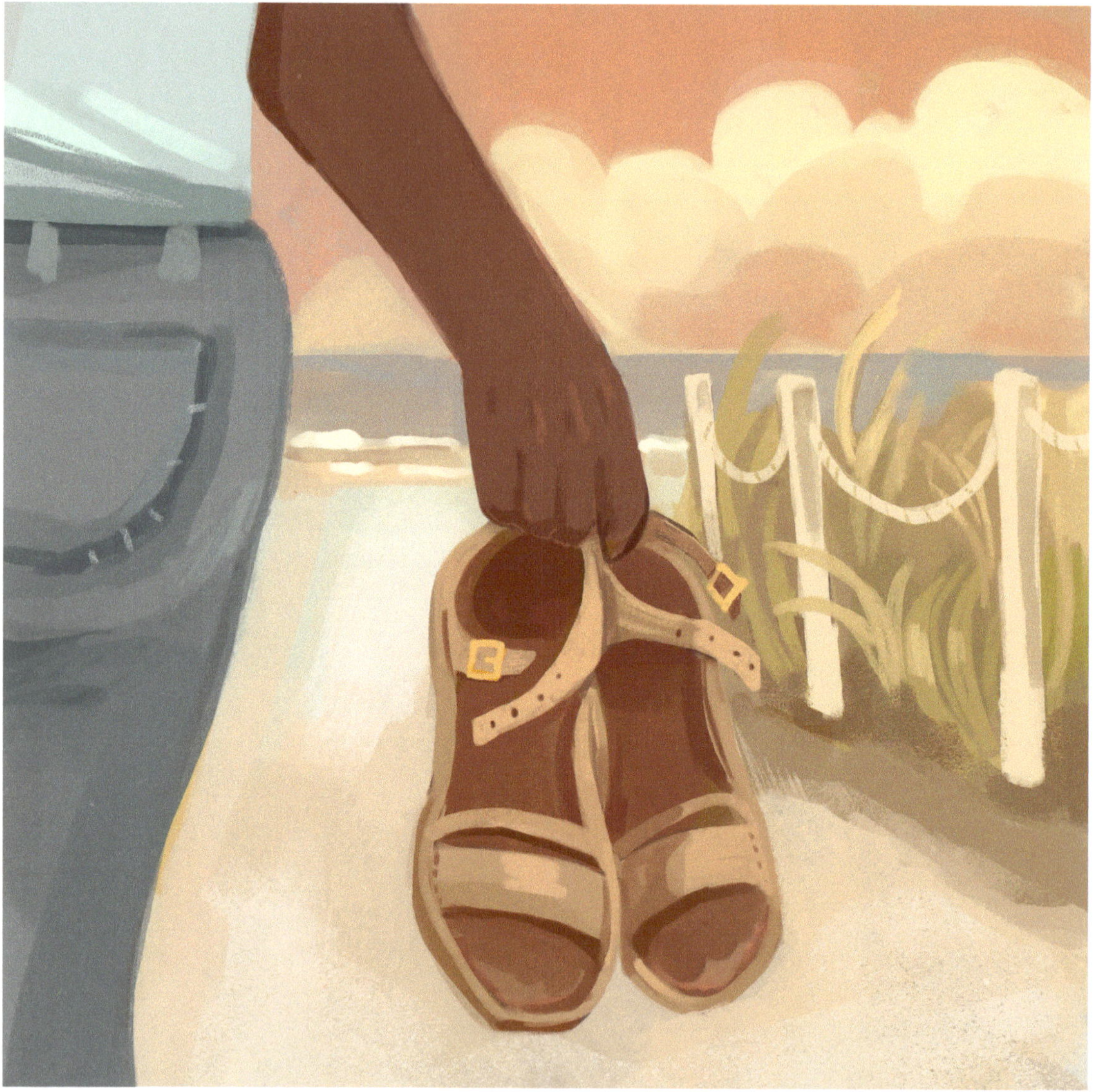

46

Help them with sandals or buckles

Famously, Prince Charming put the glass slipper on Cinderella. While most of us are not royalty, we can treat our partners as if they were, by buckling or tying shoes or sandals that are difficult to fasten. The new ones are especially stiff, and some of the straps are skinny. Another set of hands makes getting dressed (or undressed) a lot more romantic.

47

Make them a birthday or anniversary coupon

Having a blank on what to get for your partner for that special day? Want to give something playful? Create a Birthday or Anniversary Coupon! Make it on your computer or by hand, and give it to them in an envelope. Offer to do something for them, like doing the dishes for a month, getting their jewelry repaired, or seeing a movie they want to see. Put on an expiration date (like "Good for One Month"), so they don't wait to redeem it.

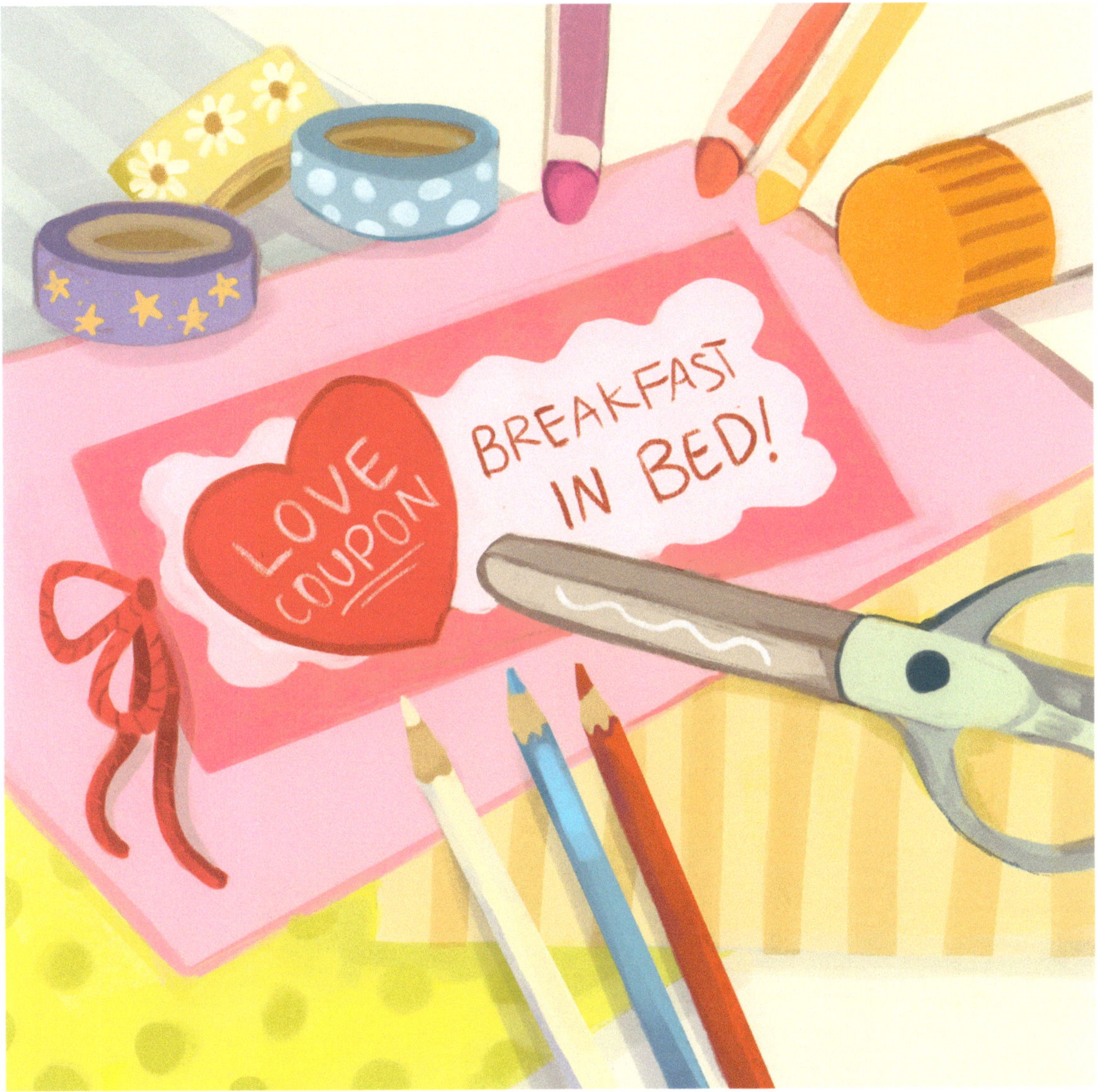
LOVE COUPON
BREAKFAST IN BED!

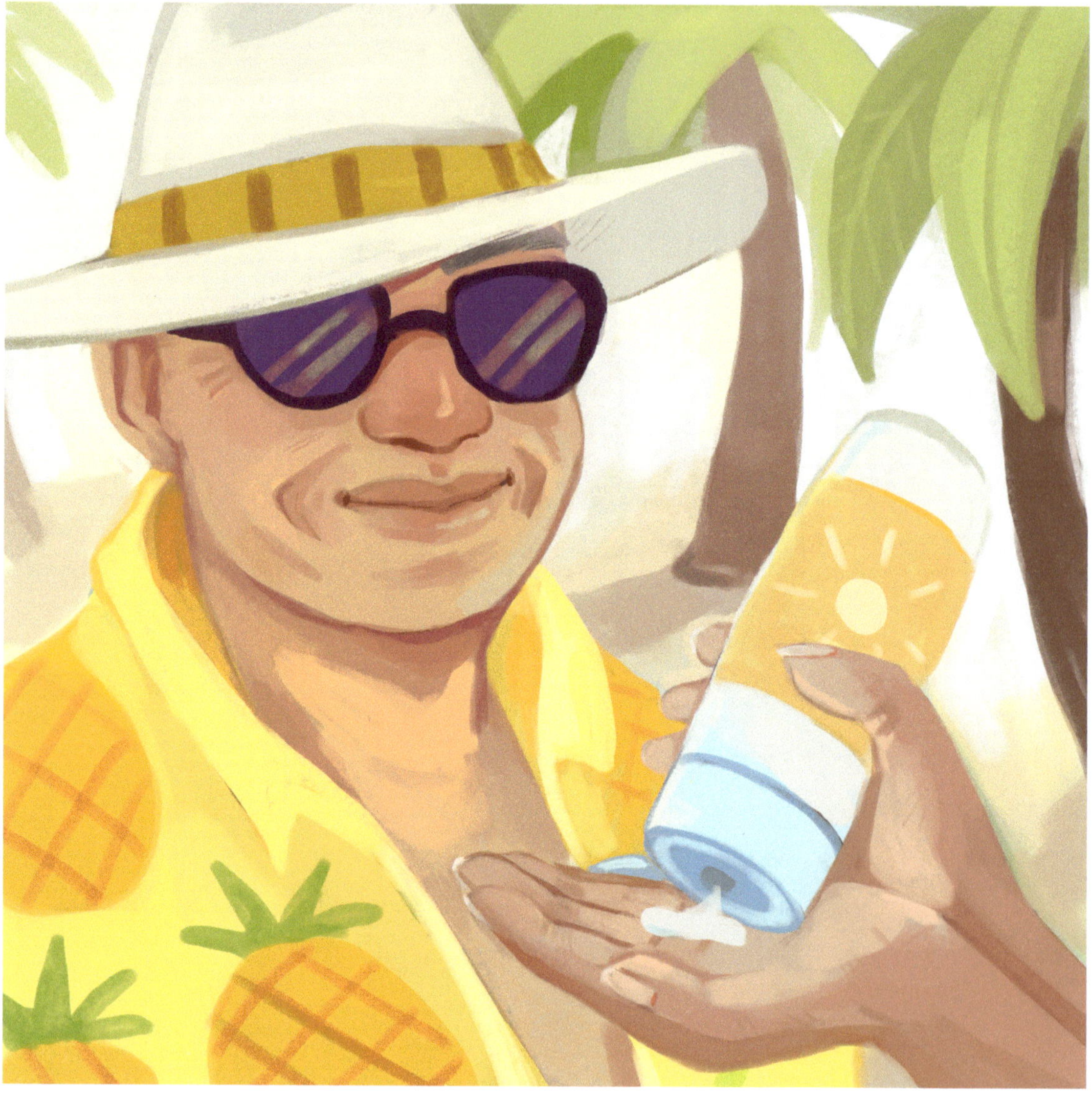

48

Protect their skin

If you spend any time in the sun—in the car, mowing the lawn, gardening, or walking—you're likely being exposed to sun. Those interested in decreasing dark spots, wrinkles, or sunburn can benefit from wearing sunscreen. Protect your partner's face, ears, hands, feet, and neck when they are going outside—especially parts they can't reach themselves, in a mini-massage to even out coverage.

49

Spend time together in nature

Share the wonder of the outdoors! Try running and laughing by the water, walking on a wooded trail, having a picnic, swimming in a pond, making a snow angel, canoeing, jumping in leaf piles, sledding, or snow skiing. Wordless walking, taking in the beauty, is hard to surpass for relaxation and feeling close. We spend so much time indoors and connected to technology, being outside and "out of range" with someone you love is a rare pleasure.

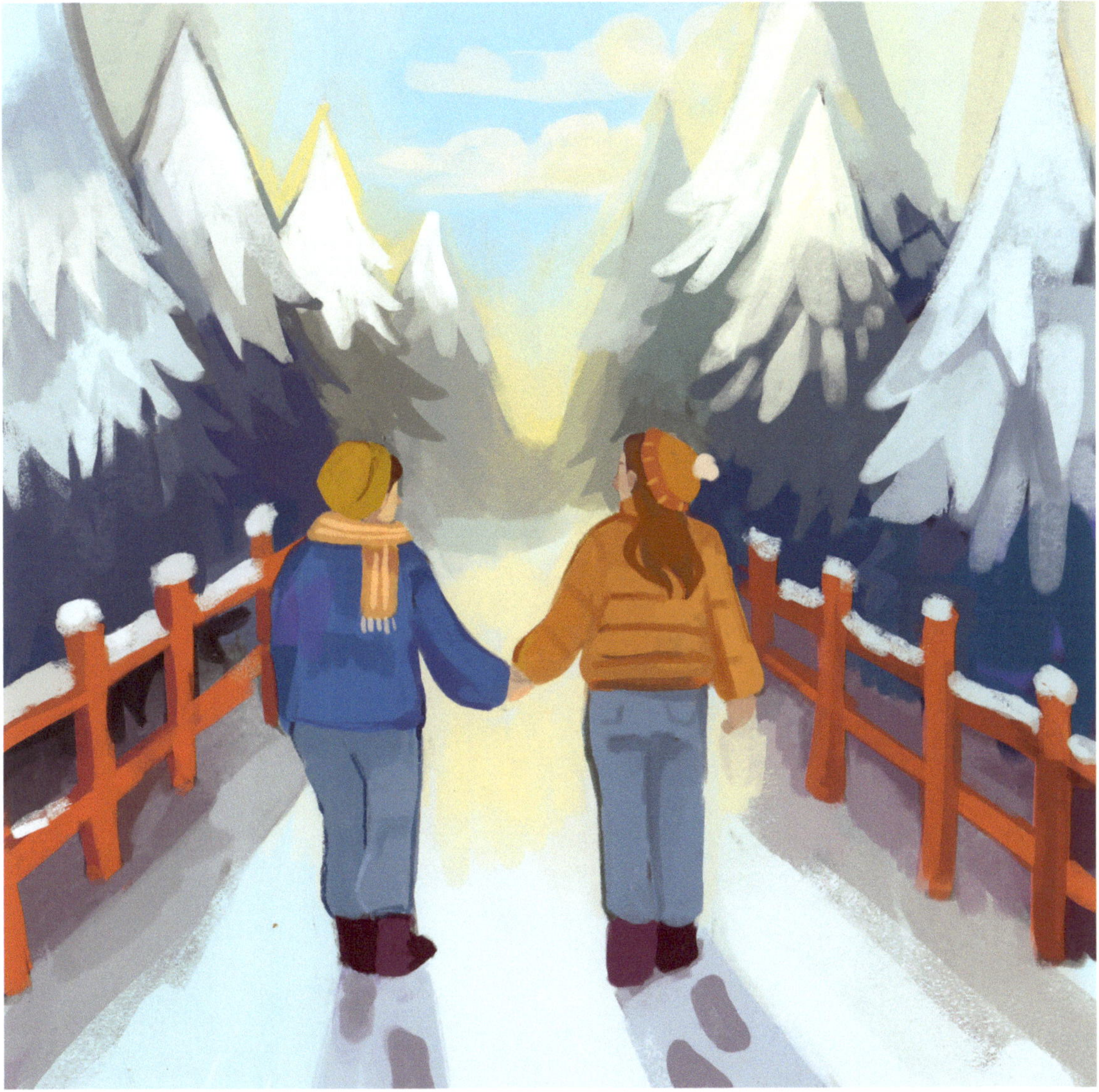

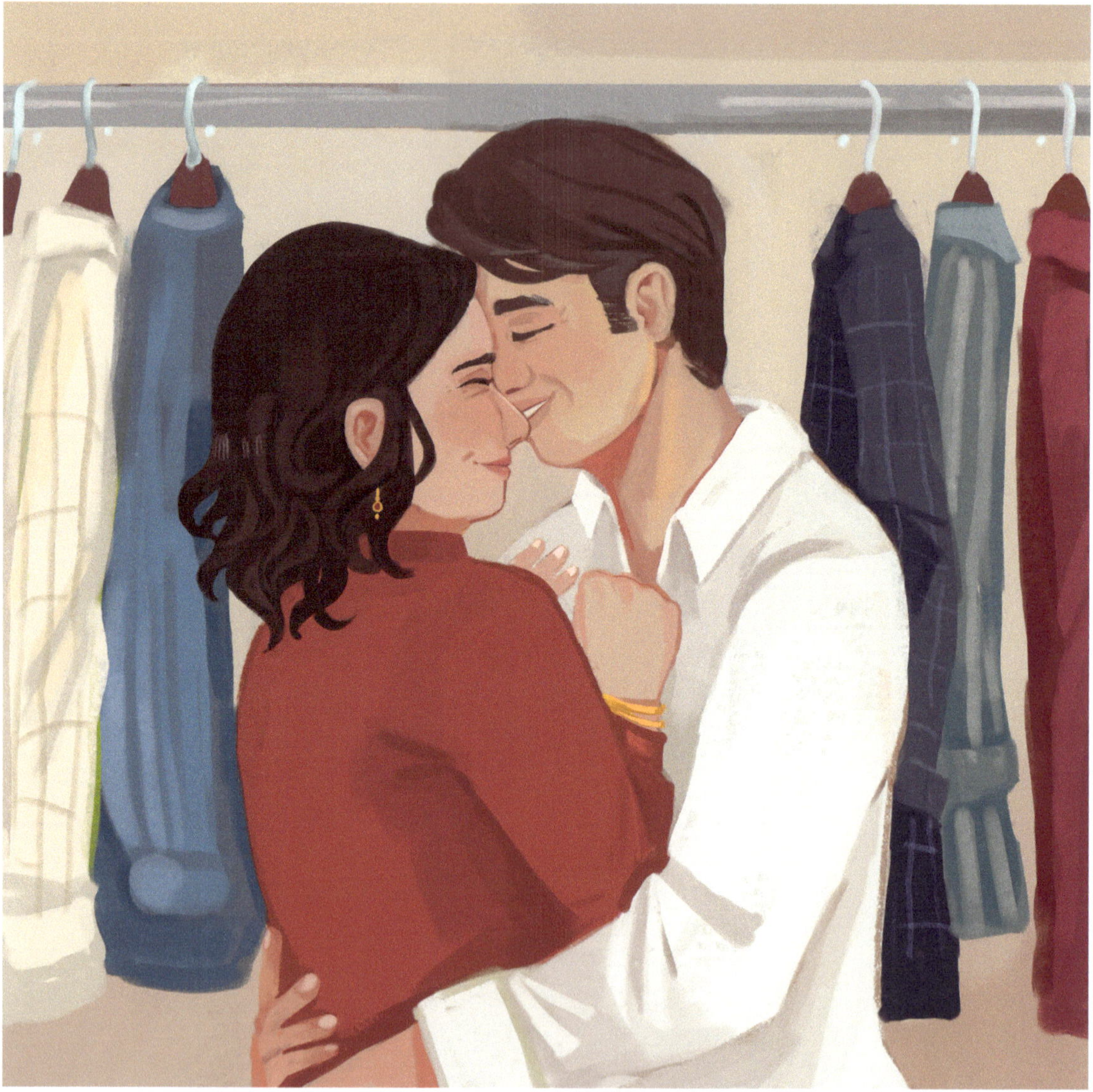

50

Give them a 15-second hug

You'd be surprised how long that is. Try it first with a timer—your watch with a second hand, while the microwave is cooking, or the last few seconds when the washing machine is spinning. Feel your bodies relax into each other, let out a deep breath... Ahhh. Then hug a little tighter before you release. When you do it often enough, you won't need a timer and can steal 15-second hugs anywhere, even in the closet!

51

Provide "Personal Cliff Notes®"

Not all of us enjoy reading or have the time to read. Many of us, however, want to know the plotline of popular book that people are talking about. If one of the partners enjoys reading, he or she can provide "Personal Cliff Notes®" to the other—a summary of books to save each other time. My husband calls it "literary cheating" but I call these sharing moments "efficient." Either way, knowing a book's contents offers another point of connection if they are brought up in your conversations.

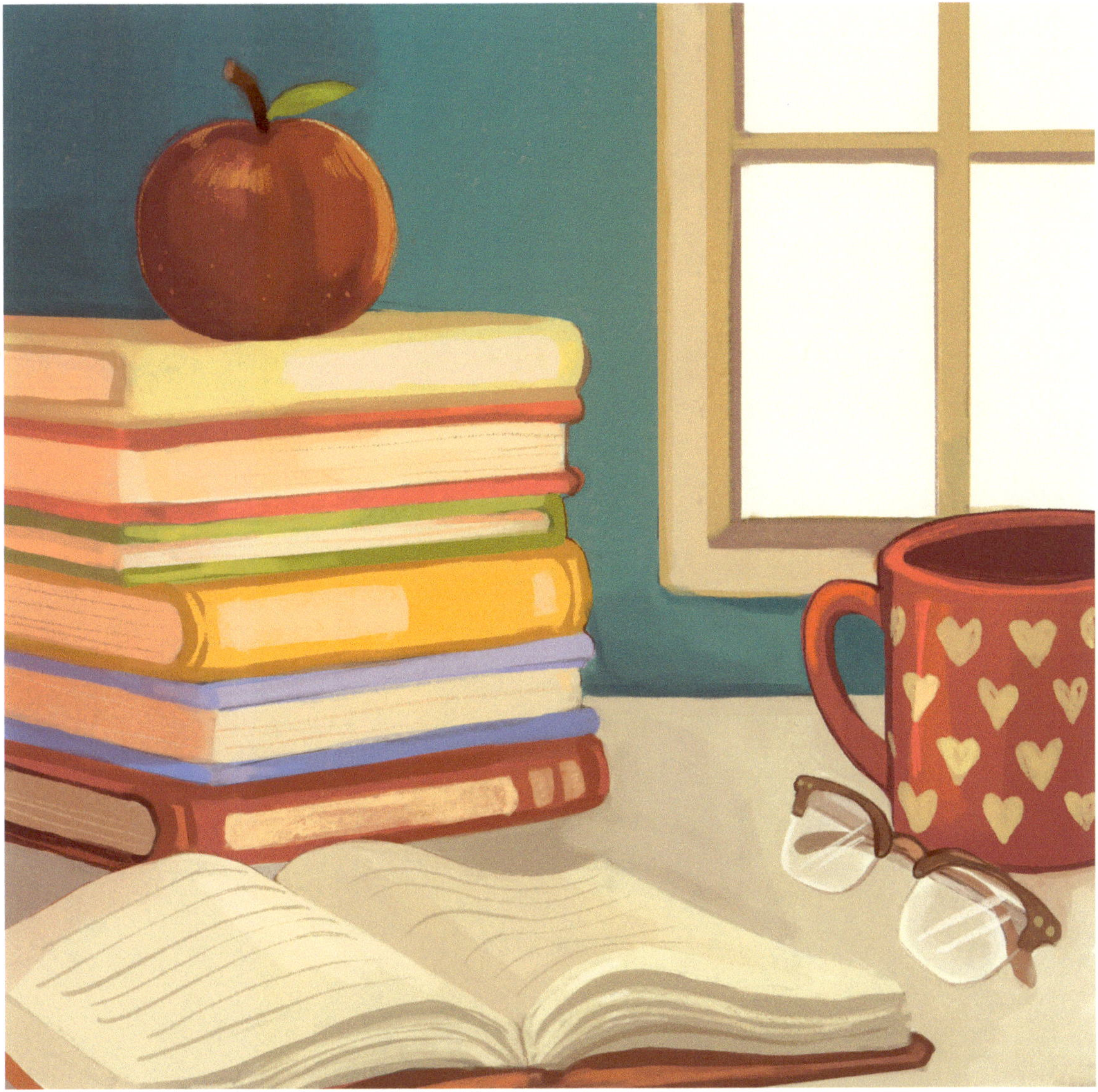

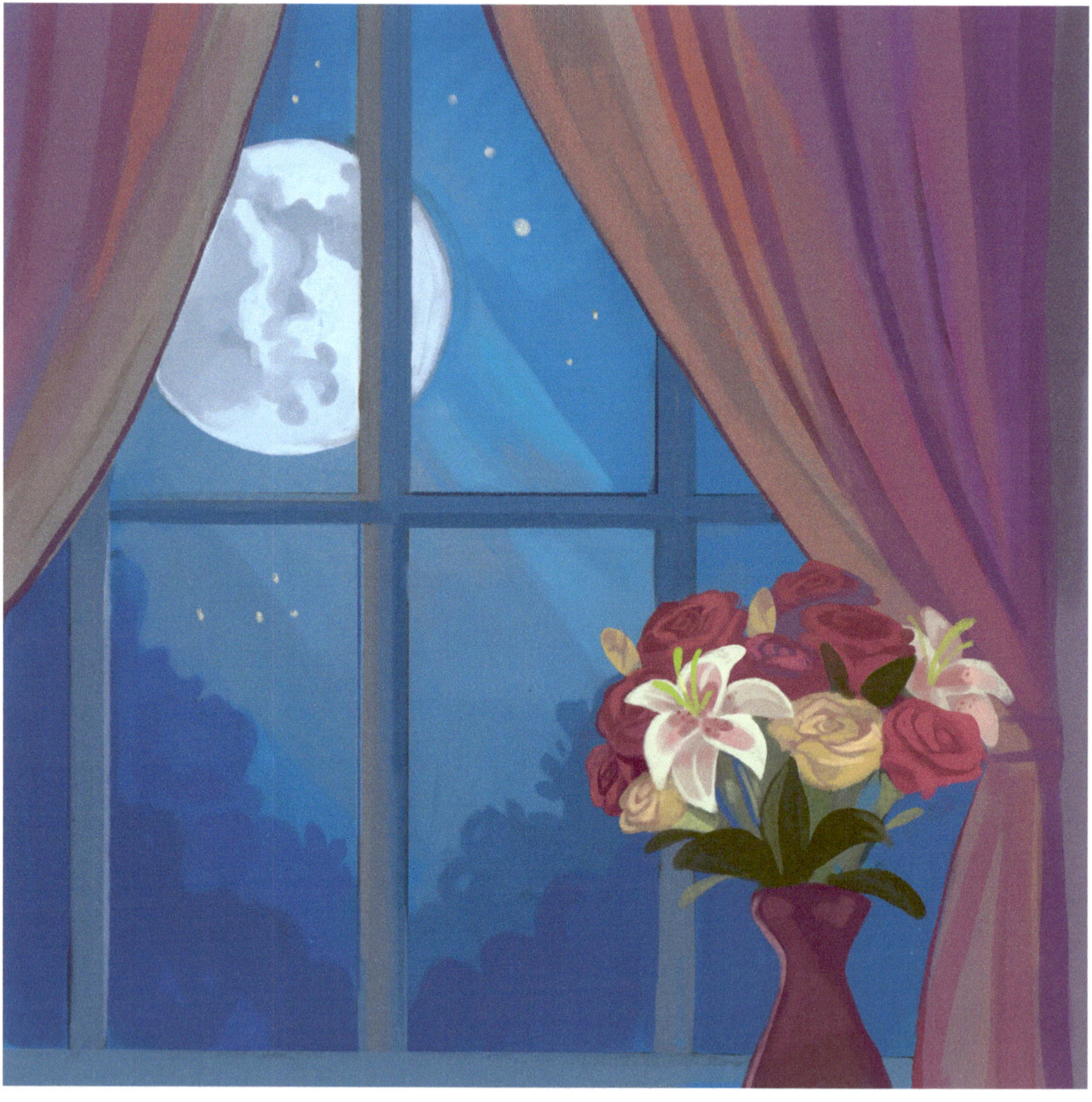

52

Say "I love you. Good night"

Before sleeping, end your day together with simple little acts. Say "I love you. Good night" and kiss them. Then listen to their heartbeat and their breathing. No matter how frustrated or angry you may have been with them earlier, be thankful every night for this beautiful partner sharing your life and your love.

About the Author

A lifelong learner and writer, Bonnie B. Daneker has been part of the publishing industry for more than 20 years. She established Georgia's first publishing advisory firm to help clients write books and has managed over 100 book-content projects.

Before her time in publishing, she worked in technology consulting. Bonnie holds a BA in Journalism from The Ohio State University, an MBA in Strategic Planning and Entrepreneurship from The Goizueta Business School at Emory University, and the Sustainability Associate Certification from ISSP. She has instructed at Savannah College of Art and Design (SCAD) and guest-lectured at Emory University. Bonnie lives with her husband outside Dallas, TX.

Visit her website at www.TheAuthorsGreenhouse.com

About the Illustrator

A "digital painter," Eevie Lanier is a book and visual development illustrator. She has done work for Square Panda and Stride educational video games.

Eevie is a graduate of Savannah College of Art and Design(SCAD) with a BFA in Illustration with a Concentration in Concept Design for Animation and Games. Previously, she graduated from the Alabama School of Fine Arts. She lives in Birmingham, AL with her two dogs and one cat. Her corgi Honey was the inspiration for the "Rub Their Belly" illustration in this book.

She can be reached through LinkedIn at: www.linkedin.com/in/Eevie-Lanier.

More from
Bonnie B. Daneker:

Stoplights Are For Laughing

Stoplights Are For Singing

Leave a Review!

As a self-published author, reviews mean the world!
Please leave a review on the platform from which
you purchased this book. I read every one!

www.ingramcontent.com/pod-product-compliance
Lightning Source LLC
Chambersburg PA
CBHW041239020426
42333CB00002B/22